Running IN FLORIDA

Notice: This book should be used as a reference guide only, not as a medical manual. The information provided here is intended to help you learn about the sport of running. The author offers his opinion and personal experience to help you may make an informed decision about your running and fitness program. This book is not written as a substitute for any professional medical or fitness advice. As with any fitness program, please check with your doctor before participating. Neither the author nor the publisher will assume responsibility for accidents or injuries that occur while engaging in any of the activities outlined in this book.

Indian River Drive, Cocoa

Running IN FLORIDA

A PRACTICAL GUIDE FOR RUNNERS IN THE SUNSHINE STATE

Mauricio Herreros

Pineapple Press, Inc.
Sarasota, Florida

*This book is dedicated to Lorrie, Sara, Christian, and Jonathan.
They are the light of my life. And to all the children of the world,
who bring love, innocence, and hope to us all.*

Inquiries should be addressed to:

Pineapple Press, Inc.
P.O. Box 3889
Sarasota, Florida 34230
www.pineapplepress.com

All photos by the author

Library of Congress Cataloging-in-Publication Data

Herreros, Mauricio, 1963–.
Running in Florida: a practical guide for runners in the sunshine state /
Mauricio Herreros— 1st ed.
cm.
    Includes bibliographical references and index.
    ISBN 1-56164-273-8 (pbk. : alk. paper)
        1. Running—Florida—Guidebooks. 2. Marathon running—
Florida—Guidebooks. 3. Florida—Guidebooks. I. Title.

GV1061.22.F56 H47 2002
796.42'09759—dc21

                                                    2002152278

First Edition
10 9 8 7 6 5 4 3 2 1

Design by Shé Sicks
Printed in the United States of America

Also by Mauricio Herreros: *Simply Running: An Inspirational and
Common Sense Guide to Running*

ACKNOWLEDGMENTS

I want to thank my wife Lorrie for her invaluable support of this project. She edited and reviewed each chapter innumerable times, always with a smile and much encouragement. I am especially thankful to my kids for their true love and kindness in allowing me to spend countless hours on this book and not with them.

Many thanks to the following people for their invaluable contributions: Doug Alred, Charlie Powell, Ken Bendy, and the 1st Place Sports store staff (Jacksonville), Joe Edgecombe (Panama City), Sharon Hunt (Pensacola), Leslie Doucette (St. Augustine), Cynthia and Bob Barnard (Ft. Lauderdale), George Dondanville (Naples), Bonita Sorensen and Len Koch (Daytona Beach), Rebecca Sparks (Cocoa Beach), Marty Winkel (Titusville), Denise Canina (Melbourne), Dr. Matt Werd (Lakeland), Andre Raveling (Gainesville), Mike Melton (Stuart), Renee Blaney (Ocala), Linda Schumacher (Clearwater), Tom Chambers (Sarasota), Carolyn Wetzel (Fort Myers), Reid Shilton, and the Fast Feet store staff (Fort Myers), the Running Center store staff (Tampa), Jay (Palm Beach), Carol Virga (Boca Raton), Jim Smith, and Donald J. Nelson (Florida Keys). Without their input this would not be a complete work.

Special thanks to two people who went out of their way to help with this project: Mary Ramba and Marlene White (Melbourne). Thanks for always answering all my questions.

June and David Cussen, my patient publishers, editor Alba Aragón, and the rest of the dedicated staff at Pineapple Press, thank you all for your support throughout this undertaking.

Finally, I would like to thank my parents Humberto and Patricia for a lifetime of love and friendship.

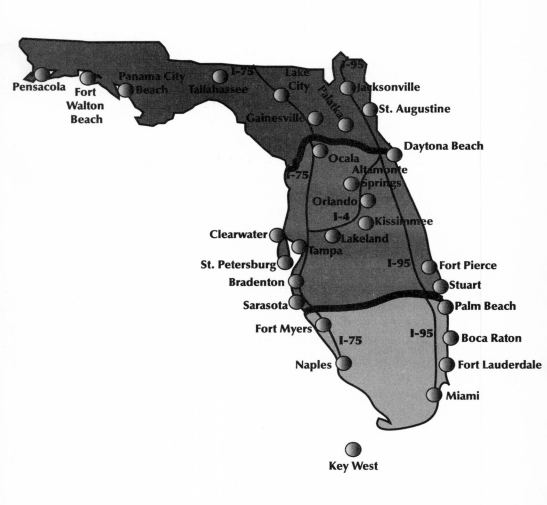

Pensacola

Fort
Walton
Beach

Panama City
Beach

Tallahassee

I-75

Lake
City

I-95

Jacksonville

Palatka

St. Augustine

Gainesville

Daytona Beach

Ocala

I-75

Altamonte
Springs

Orlando

I-4

Kissimmee

Clearwater

Lakeland

Tampa

St. Petersburg

I-95

Fort Pierce

Bradenton

Stuart

Sarasota

Palm Beach

Fort Myers

I-75

I-95

Boca Raton

Naples

Fort Lauderdale

Miami

Key West

CONTENTS

Run on hard, packed sand, Miami Beach.

INTRODUCTION

Whether you are visiting the Sunshine State or already live here, *Running in Florida* can be a valuable companion for any runner looking to enhance his/her Florida running experience. The best places to run, the coolest races, and what the running scene is like in each region are just a few of the topics covered. This book is loaded with practical information to help you discover the best running in Florida.

The truth is that there is no other place like the Sunshine State, with its excellent year-round weather, beautiful outdoor scenery, and almost endless running options. Living and running in Florida for more than a decade, I have experienced the best of this runner's paradise firsthand. And now, with *Running in Florida,* you can too.

HOW TO USE THIS BOOK

For easy reference, *Running in Florida* has been divided into three sections, which correspond to the three main geographical regions of the state.

North Florida
Central Florida
South Florida

Each section includes the major cities and towns in that region. There are twenty-one featured cities in all. Within each area the information provided follows these categories:

Description of the Area
Best Places to Run
Best Local Races
Running Clubs
Other Resources

Because it was not possible to include every place to run and every road race in Florida, the following criteria were used to select the best running places and races in the state:

BEST PLACES TO RUN: Several factors were considered when choosing the best places to run, including safety, location, accessibility, parking availability, and popularity with local runners. For each of the running places selected, a description of the area is provided along with directions, approximate mileage, and possible expectations in terms of facilities, terrain, and so on. Because it was not practical to include maps for each of the 147 featured runs, the directions offered assume that you will use a local map in addition to this guide. This section is organized in alphabetical order.

BEST LOCAL RACES: Some of the criteria used for selecting the 159 featured road races were uniqueness of the event, popularity, location, and whether it was an established race (at least five years old). The information provided for each selected race includes a description of the event and its location, the month when it is held, and generally what to expect. No specific dates or entry forms are provided, since this information changes slightly from year to year. For specific dates and entry forms contact the running stores and/or running clubs in your area of interest (see references at the end of each section) or check the various online calendars available (see Resources, p. 168). This section is organized in chronological order.

Additionally, each featured area contains two reference categories:

RUNNING CLUBS: Although in Florida the majority of running clubs are members of the Road Runners Club of America (RRCA), there are a few well-organized clubs that are not. Here you will find both types of running clubs.

OTHER RESOURCES: This section contains a useful bundle of information about each featured area and its vicinity, including any running stores and a number of websites that provide practical information about the location (such as the local newspaper, county, city, visitors' bureau, etc.).

Though every effort has been made to provide up-to-date and accurate information, keep in mind that changes will take place. When in doubt, make sure to contact the appropriate persons or places to avoid disappointment.

A FEW COMMON-SENSE RUNNING TIPS

Here is a list of some basic rules to keep in mind when running in Florida or elsewhere:

☺ Always choose sidewalks over roads when available. Watch for pedestrians.

- Avoid running in high traffic areas such as busy roads and high-ways.
- Watch for traffic, especially at street intersections and crossings.
- Always carry identification and some cash for emergencies.
- Run during daylight hours. The best times are usually early in the morning or later in the afternoon. Avoid the hottest time of day, especially in the summer.
- Never run outdoors when there is lightning in the area. If caught outside during a lightning storm, seek shelter immediately. Avoid trees and open spaces. As a last resort, lie down on the ground.
- When running in state parks, trails, or isolated areas:
    - Avoid running alone, especially after sundown. Instead, run with a partner or in a group.
    - Let others know where you are going and when you should be expected back.
    - Get a map of the area to orient yourself.
    - Watch for uneven terrain that may cause you to fall or sprain your foot.
    - If possible, carry a cellular phone for emergencies.
    - If running with a dog, make sure to bring a leash (required at most parks).
    - Lock valuables out of sight in your car to avoid break-ins.
    - Be aware of bikes and pedestrians in the area.
    - Apply insect repellent, especially in wooded areas.
    - Respect wildlife. Leave only footprints behind.
- When preparing to run in an unfamiliar place, ask local runners for tips. If possible, drive around the area first and check the route you will be running.
- Dress for the occasion. On hot days wear light-colored clothing that absorbs less heat. Wear reflective gear for evening and early morning runs. Wear sunscreen to protect your skin from the harsh Florida sun.
- Always drink plenty of water before and after a run. Bring water along, especially if you will be going for a long run. Stay hydrated. Don't use thirst as an indicator—by then you will be already dehydrated.
- Avoid running on very hot and humid days if you are sensitive to heat or are taking prescription medicine. Don't push yourself on hot days.

- Pay attention to signs of heat problems. Stop running if you feel dizzy, confused, or nauseous; or if you sweat excessively or observe any unusual symptoms. If you experience any of the above, consult with your doctor before running again.
- Always listen to your body for signs of problems. Stop running if something doesn't feel right. Ask for help if necessary.
- When running outdoors, consider leaving behind your portable CD-player or radio. Instead, listen to the sounds of nature.

The key to a long-lasting and pleasurable running experience is to use common sense. Give your body a break sometimes. Remember that we are not machines. Allow rest days between runs and never run while sick. Keep running simple and natural. Always put personal safety and well-being first. Avoid unnecessary risks. Relax and enjoy.

NORTH FLORIDA

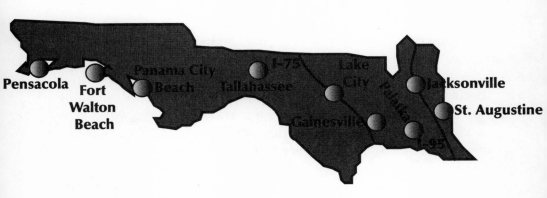

Pensacola

Fort
Walton
Beach

Panama City
Beach

Tallahassee

I-75

Lake
City

Jacksonville

Palatka

St. Augustine

Gainesville

I-95

North Florida, the biggest region in the state, extends for more than 370 miles from the blue waters of the Atlantic Ocean to the state line west of Pensacola. Compared with the rest of Florida, this vast area is the least populated and perhaps the most geographically diverse, with hundreds of rivers, swamps, lakes, forests, and unspoiled beaches. The landscape on the east is flat and sandy near the coast, with gentle higher ground inland. Moving west, rolling hills abound, including Walton County's Britton Hill, which is the highest elevation point in the state at 345 feet. You will also find some steep bluffs along rivers and coastal areas.

The climate is cooler than in the rest of Florida. While summer temperatures are hot, spring and fall are much milder seasons. But the most noticeable change happens during the winter months, when temperatures fall to the 40°s. Although snow is very rare, much colder temperatures are not uncommon, but these usually don't last long, with sudden swings within a few hours. In a way North Florida, with its huge forests, tall trees, small hills, and marked seasons, has more similarities with southern Georgia and Alabama than with the rest of Florida. But this is what makes this region so unique and beautiful and offers endless opportunities for outdoor activities the whole year.

Runners visiting or living in this friendly region will find a huge and varied number of places to run, including some of the best nature trails in Florida, state parks, beautiful residential areas, historic neighborhoods, scenic bridges, and tens of miles of pristine beaches along both the Atlantic Ocean and the Gulf of Mexico. The running scene in North Florida is tremendously active, with many well-established and organized running clubs hosting dozens of running events throughout the year including several nationally recognized road races.

Running is a year-round activity in North Florida. This is confirmed by the thousands of runners that live and run in the major cities and towns of this region every day. The possibilities are limitless. Jacksonville, St. Augustine, Palatka, Gainesville, Tallahassee, Panama City, Fort Walton Beach, and Pensacola represent the major running centers of North Florida. In the following pages I have included some of the best places to run, best road races, and most useful reference information about each of the featured running areas.

JACKSONVILLE AREA

Jacksonville is the largest city in Florida and home to the Gate River Run, the 15K US National Championship. Located along the Atlantic Ocean and St. Johns River, this up-and-coming city has over 840 square miles of mostly flat terrain. Here you will find many places to run—beautiful beaches, parks, nature trails, residential areas, roads, and bridges. The running community is big and very active. There are several well-established running clubs and specialty running stores. The list of local races is extensive and always growing. No matter what time of year, there are likely to be several race events held during each month. With so many running options, it is no surprise that Jacksonville has become a favorite place for thousands of runners around the state.

BEST PLACES TO RUN

Avondale/Riverside Area: This beautiful residential neighborhood near the downtown area is located on the west side of the St. Johns River. Riverside Avenue and St. Johns Avenue are two of the main streets. Here you will see many historic homes along the shaded streets. Run on the sidewalk and watch for cars.

Black Creek Trail: This is a pleasant seven-mile trail along the west side of US 17 from the Doctors Lake Bridge south of Orange Park to the Black Creek Trail area. Most of the trail is paved, but there is a long wooden bridge section over a low portion of the trail adjacent to US 17. If you decide to drive to the trail, the best way is to go to the south end, which is located on US 17 about ten miles south of I-295, right north of the Black Creek Bridge. There you will find a parking lot and a water fountain. From this point you can run north on the trail and back. There are some markers along the way to help you track your distance. Bring water along if you decide to go for a long run. The trail is closed at sundown.

Bolles High School Track: This is a great place to do speed training. Bolles has a well-maintained, full-size synthetic track, a treat for

US 17 Black Creek Trail, Orange Park

your feet. The track is open to local runners once a week, usually Wednesday evenings. Since this is a private school, the best thing is to check the track's schedule with the school by calling (904) 733-9292, or ask the friendly staff at the1st Place Sports running store.

Camp Tomahawk Park: This is a small but beautiful park located in the San Jose area a few blocks from the Jewish Community Alliance club. Driving from San Jose Boulevard turn into San Clerc Road. Continue until San Ardo Drive and make a left. Keep going until you see the park's entrance. This park has a couple of softball fields, a shaded playground, and a nature trail. The loop around the park is less than a mile long. Water and restrooms are available behind the picnic area. This is a nice place to let the kids play while you run around the nature trail and fields.

District 2 Regional Park: This is the old Dunes Golf Course which has been converted into a city park. It is located in Arlington between Monument and McCormick roads. The main entrance is off McCormick Road about a quarter of a mile from Monument Road. The area has lots of grass fields to walk or run on and a shaded trail around the park. There is a paved road going from the main entrance to the side entrance by Monument Road. Parking, restrooms and water are available inside the park.

Doctors Lake Trail: This is a beautiful paved trail located in Orange Park along Doctors Lake Road. The 4.5-mile trail starts at Kingsley Avenue and ends on Peoria Road. Most of the trail is shaded, with some steep areas. There are mile markers on the pavement for reference. This is one of the most scenic runs in Jacksonville and a great place to get some hill training in a mostly flat city. Bring water since there are no facilities along the way.

Downtown Bridges Loop: Starting at Museum Circle in front of the MOSH (Museum of Science and History), run toward the Main Street Bridge. Go over the Main Street Bridge. As you descend the bridge, bear left. You will be on Independent Drive. Run past the Jacksonville Landing. Soon after, the street name will change to Water Street. Continue straight all the way until you get to the Acosta Bridge. Go over the Acosta Bridge toward San Marco Boulevard and swerve left, back to the MOSH circle. The loop is about 1.8 miles long. Repeat as many loops as desired. There is drinking water avail-

Running down the Main Street Bridge, Jacksonville

able by the Friendship Fountain between the St Johns River and the north side of the MOSH. Be aware that the Acosta Bridge has an elevation grade of six to seven percent. This means that the road rises six to seven feet every one hundred feet. This is a high grade, so be careful if you have never run uphill before. The Main Street Bridge is a little less than half a mile long. The Acosta Bridge is about a mile long. Run this loop in both directions to get a more balanced muscle workout.

Florida Community College at Jacksonville–North Campus: Located on Capper Road in a quiet residential area on the north side of Jacksonville, the FCCJ campus has a beautiful shaded trail with live oak and pine trees. This is a great place to do some trail training. Several cross-country races are held on this campus during the fall. Many local runners believe that this is one of Jacksonville's best-kept running secrets.

Jacksonville–Baldwin Trail: This is one of the best runs in Jacksonville. It is an old railroad line that was converted into a recreational 14.5-mile trail between Imeson Road in Jacksonville and County Road 121 west of Baldwin. The trail is paved and is open to joggers, cyclists, skaters, and hikers. This is a great place to go for a scenic quiet run or to train for longer distances. Before venturing onto this tree-lined trail consider how far you plan to go. You may want to use time as your guide. For example, run for forty-five minutes in and then turn back. The Jacksonville trailhead is located on Imeson Road about 1.2 miles west of I-295. Take I-295 to Commonwealth Avenue, and go west on Commonwealth Avenue to Imeson Road. Imeson Road is less than a mile from the interstate exit. You should see an industrial area, and go over the railroad tracks. Turn on Imeson Road and the trail's entrance is less than half a mile on your left. There is plenty of parking and a couple of portable restrooms by the entrance. There is no water available, so bring your own. The trail is maintained by the city of Jacksonville. For more information, call (904) 630-4100 or visit www.coj.net.

Jacksonville Beaches Area: Here you will find many miles of beautiful, white, packed-sand beach between Ponte Vedra and Mayport. A great place to run is Jacksonville Beach by the Seawalk Pavilion. This is located at the end of Beach Boulevard (US 90) and First Street. When you get to First Street make a left and the pavilion is one block up on your right. There is plenty of free parking across the street. Several popular beach races start and finish here. From this point you can run for several miles north or south. A beach run is always high on my list, and Jacksonville Beach is one of my favorites. The best times to run are early in the morning or late in the afternoon. Remember to wear sunscreen and to hydrate.

Jacksonville University: Located on University Boulevard and Merrill Road, this beautiful campus has shaded, rolling trails and a small but challenging hill. Watch for cars and walkers. The loop around the campus is 1.5 miles.

Kathryn Abbey Hanna Park: Located south of the Mayport Naval Base, this oceanfront park offers a great range of options. Here you will find a 1.5-mile beach stretch and several miles of scenic nature trails which can be quite challenging at various points. If you run the trails watch for bikes, wildlife, and tree roots. There are restrooms and water by the entrance. The park is open daily from 8 A.M. to sundown. A small admission fee is required. For more information call the park administration at (904) 249-4700. The entrance to the park is on Wonderwood Drive off Mayport Road.

Mandarin Park: This is a city park located near the south end of Mandarin Road about 0.3 miles from San Jose Boulevard. The park has tennis courts, a playground, picnic areas, several nature trails, and a dock on Julington Creek. The main trail loop is 1.7 miles long. Water and restrooms are available by the playground area. The park is free and open daily from 5 A.M. to sundown. This is a great place for a scenic and easy run.

Ortega Area: This is a beautiful residential area surrounded on three sides by route US 17, the Ortega River, and the St. Johns River. This area has plenty of shaded streets to run on. Watch for cars, especially if you run along US 17 and over the Roosevelt Bridge. Ortega Boulevard ends on Timuquana Road, which connects US 17 with Blanding Boulevard. There are sidewalks along most of the main roads.

River Road: Located in Orange Park about a mile south of the Naval Air Station Jacksonville, this is a scenic area with a view of the St. Johns river. Start on River Road by the Orange Park Kennel Club (Wells Road) and run south towards Kingsley Avenue. The run is about 1.5 miles each way.

San Jose Boulevard: This scenic tree-lined road is also known as State Road 13. It starts near the San Marco area and goes south for miles, crossing many neighborhoods through Jacksonville to northern St. Johns County. This road is so long that you could almost complete a marathon if you started at one end and ran to the other end and back. There are sidewalks along a big portion of the boulevard, but this is not the case with most of the side streets that converge into it. For an easy run, start in front of the Bolles School at the corner of Santa Barbara Street and head south on San Jose Boulevard. Stay on the southbound sidewalk. Keep going straight up to Holly Grove/Baymeadows Road and run back towards the start. This loop is 4.2 miles. San Jose Boulevard is a busy road, so try to avoid running during rush hours. Bring water along.

San Marco Area: This charming and stylish residential and commercial area is close to downtown. San Marco Boulevard, the main road, has several blocks of trendy shops and restaurants. San Marco Boulevard merges into Hendricks Avenue. On River Road you get a view of the St. Johns River before turning into a charming residential neighborhood. There are sidewalks along most streets in the area. Watch for pedestrians, bicycles and cars. The annual 15K River Run course runs through part of this neighborhood. There is a loop of about three miles beginning from San Marco Boulevard through Laverne Street, River Road, River Oaks Road, Hendricks Avenue, and back to San Marco Boulevard.

University of North Florida: Located on St. John's Bluff Road about one mile north of J. Turner Butler Boulevard (JTB), UNF offers several nature trails of various lengths. The paved loop around the main campus is about two miles. If running on the road, make sure to watch for traffic. The university has a track available, which is usually open to all runners. The track is located next to the tennis courts and the indoor swimming pool. Water and restrooms are available. There is a small parking fee for visitors.

Van Zant Park: This rural park is located on Sandridge Road in Middleburg near Lake Asbury. There is a sand-and-dirt trail around the park of about 1.5 miles. There are several grass fields, picnic areas and a small lagoon. This is a nice place to go for an authentic Florida trail run, but the loose sand can be tough. The park has restrooms and plenty of parking. If you decide to venture there, make sure to bring a Clay County map since the park can be hard to find if you are not familiar with the area. As always, it is safer to run with a friend. Bring water along.

Westside Regional Park: This city park is located on US 17 across from the Yorktown entrance to Naval Air Station Jacksonville. There are two miles of paved road and several dirt trails. The park is very shaded and serene. There are picnic tables, a playground, restrooms, water and an archery range. The park is open daily from 5 A.M. to sundown.

BEST LOCAL RACES

Winter Beaches Runs 5M and 10M: This double race is a popular event in North Florida. It is held in February in Jacksonville Beach. Both distances start together and go along the beach. This can be a tough race, especially for beginners or people who are not used to running on sand. Sometimes the weather can be windy and cold, or just perfect for running. If you want a little challenge this is a great race. Start with the five-miler if you are a beginner or have never run on sand.

Ortega River Run 5M: This popular race is held in mid-February. The five-mile course goes through the scenic and tree-lined streets of the Ortega neighborhood including the Roosevelt Bridge on US 17. The race starts and finishes on Ortega Boulevard in front of St. Marks Episcopal School. This event offers plenty of challenge because of its length and the bridge, making it a nice stepping stone for runners training for the 15K River Run. The post-race party is fun, with lots of good food and the good company of fellow runners.

Gate River Run 15K : Held in early March, the Jacksonville 15K River Run is the largest and best-organized running event in Northeast Florida. It is the National 15K Championship and brings several of the country's elite runners. Each year almost ten thousand competitors of all abilities gather in Jacksonville's downtown area for this popular race. Two days prior to the 15K event a large runner's Expo is held through race day. This is a good place to find top quality running merchandise at discount prices. The River Run is a definite challenge for any runner. With two big bridges and a 9.3-mile course, this race is no joke. Aside from being a tough event, it is an awesome experience. The sight of thousands of runners lined up at the start inspires many of us to return year after year. If you are a runner in North Florida, this is a race you don't want to miss. The post-race party is first-class with lots of food and drinks for everyone. In addition to the 15K event, the River Run has a 5K walk and a one-mile fun run for kids. All of these events add up to make this a wonderful running event for everyone.

Run to the Sun 8K: This popular event is held in April in Orange Park. The race starts in front of the Kennel Club, goes south on US 17, and then turns back through River Road to finish behind the club. The course is flat, fast, and mostly shaded. This race has a Clydesdale category for men and women. The post-race party is fun and entertaining. The Florida Striders do a great job hosting their events, and this one is no exception. I like this race because in April the weather is still nice, and I get a chance to run something longer than a 5K. This is good practice for anyone training for a 10K.

Shrimp Festival 5K: This event is held in May during the Shrimp Festival in Fernandina Beach, a small coastal town on Amelia Island north of Jacksonville. The race starts and finishes on the street side of Main Beach. The course is flat, scenic, and loops through several unpaved streets parallel to the ocean. If you are looking for a memorable run try this one. The race is great, and after the event you can head to the historic downtown area and check out the festivities. Don't forget to try the famous shrimp.

Memorial Day 5K: This traditional 5K event is held every year on Memorial Day in Green Cove Springs. The race is part of the Memorial Day Festival at Spring Park. The course is flat and fast. The race starts and finishes by the park. This 5K event attracts several hundred runners each year. There is a Clydesdale division for big runners which is a nice thing. The post-race party ceremony is held at the park. I like racing on holidays because it gets me out of the house early, and I feel energized all day after the run. This is a wonderful event for the whole family. Run, then stay for the festival activities after the race.

Run for the Pies 5K: A very popular evening race, the Run for the Pies 5K is held in early June. The course is flat and fast and starts in front of the Jacksonville Landing in downtown. The tradition at this race is to award free pies to all men and women finishing under twenty and twenty-four minutes respectively. The post-race party is at the Jacksonville Landing. There is live music, food and drinks (including beer), and free prizes. I have run this race many times, and it has usually been hot and humid, but this has not stopped me from coming back every year. What better way to spend a Saturday evening than running through downtown Jacksonville with hundreds of runners and celebrating later by the beautiful St. Johns River.

Tour de Pain: This is a unique event in North Florida, with three races in 24 hours. Held in Jacksonville in August, this challenging trio is designed to test your endurance. The first race is a four-mile run on the beach and it takes place on Friday evening. The second race is a one-mile run on the road, which takes place Saturday morning. The third and final race is a 5K run held on Saturday evening. All finishers of the three events get a medal, but you don't have to enter all three races to participate; you can enter each separately. I have run this series of races several times, and it was definitely tough. By the time you are finished with the third event you will be glad the "pain" is over. Overall, I like the challenges offered by these races. If you want to test your will and running endurance, the Tour de Pain provides just that opportunity.

Summer Beach Run 5M: This summer evening race is held at Jacksonville Beach in August. This is a popular event especially among hard-core runners. The combination of hot, humid weather and the five-mile beach course usually makes this race tough. I remember running one year when the humidity was high, the temperature was over ninety degrees, and there was no breeze. The result was that we were about to pass out. Although just finishing this race can be a real challenge, beach runs tend to inspire me and this is a nice event. The runners, the beach, and the competition make it a magical evening. The post-race party is held right there on the beach with plenty of food, drinks, and ocean for everyone after the hard run. This is a great race to experience at least once.

Autumn Fitness 5K: This traditional fall race is held during the first half of September in front of the Orange Park Kennel Club. The course is fast and very similar to the Run to the Sun 8K, except shorter. This event has a Clydesdale category, and there is a one-mile fun run after the 5K. All fun run finishers get a ribbon. This is a good reason to bring kids along and encourage them to participate and have some fun too. This is a great course for a PR time.

Outback Half-Marathon: This race is held on Thanksgiving Day in the Mandarin area of Jacksonville. The course is flat, fast, and mostly shaded, and it goes through several residential streets west of San Jose Boulevard. In recent years this event has become a classic of Northeast Florida. Several hundred runners show up every year for the 13.1-mile morning run. The race is well organized, and the post-event party is great. I like this race because it symbolizes the beginning of the holiday season. Part of the race proceeds is donated to a local food bank—a wonderful reason to enter this event, especially on Thanksgiving Day. If you plan to run a marathon in the late fall, this is definitely a race to consider since it can be a sort of stepping stone and practice before the full marathon.

Jacksonville Marathon: The Jacksonville Marathon is held in mid-December. The whole event consists of three races: the marathon, a half-marathon, and a 5K. All races start in front of Bolles School on San Jose Boulevard, but the marathon and half-marathon start before the 5K. The marathon and half-marathon course is mostly shaded and flat. The 5K course goes over the final miles of the marathon. All three events combined bring several hundred runners each year, many from out of town because the Jacksonville Marathon is one of the last qualifying marathons for the Boston Marathon. The whole event is fun, and the post-race party doesn't end at the finish line since there is a celebration party in the evening for the marathon runners. I enjoy this race because the weather is often nice, plus it helps me stay in shape through the end-of-year holidays.

RUNNING CLUBS

1st Place Sports Running Club: Founded in 1996, this is a very competitive running club. A membership fee is required join. For more information call (904) 731-3676 or write to: 1st Place Sports, 3853 Baymeadows Road, Jacksonville, FL 32217, or visit www.1stplacesports.com.

Beach Endurance Sports Team: Based in Jacksonville Beach, BEST is a group of fitness-oriented people including runners, cyclists, swimmers and walkers. Several local events are presented by this group throughout the year. A membership fee is required to join. For more information call Performance MultiSports at (904) 285-1552 or visit www.performancemultisports.com.

Florida Striders Track Club: Based in Orange Park, the club is over twenty years old. The club is very organized and family-oriented. The Striders organize weekly training groups, social events, and several popular races throughout the year. An annual membership fee is required to join. For more information visit www.floridastriders.com.

Jacksonville Track Club: Started in the 1970s, the JTC is one of the oldest and largest running clubs in North Florida. An annual membership fee is required to join. The club hosts several weekly training groups and sponsors a number of road races in Northeast Florida. For more information call (904) 384-8725 or write to: JTC, P.O. Box 24667, Jacksonville, FL 32241, or visit www.jacksonvilletrackclub.com.

OTHER RESOURCES

1st Place Sports: This running store has been in business since the late 1970s and is at the forefront of the Jacksonville running community. 1st Place Sports is a major organizer of several local races and is the best place to get the latest information on the local running scene. They offer a full line of running shoes, clothing and equipment. The store has two locations: 3853 Baymeadows Road in Jacksonville, (904) 731-3676, and at the Sand Castle Shopping Center in Jacksonville Beach, located where J. Turner Butler Boulevard meets A1A, (904) 280-3007. www.1stplacesports.com.

City of Jacksonville Official Website: Here you will find lots of good information about the community and a great visitors' guide. www.coj.net.

Florida Times-Union Online: Offers the latest local news and information about Jacksonville and surrounding areas. www.jacksonville.com.

Jacksonville and the Beaches Convention & Visitors Bureau Official Website: This is a great place to find out about Jacksonville and get useful visitor information like calendar of events, area maps, local attractions, dining, and lodging. www.jaxcvb.com.

ST. AUGUSTINE AREA

St. Augustine, the nation's oldest city, is a great place to visit and to run in year-round. Located only thirty miles south of Jacksonville, this is truly a unique city. The downtown area is perfect for a memorable run through streets filled with centuries-old historic buildings, quaint inns and picturesque shops. No other place in Florida offers runners the opportunity to see so much history in one run. Over time St. Augustine has become one of my favorite places to visit and run. Running here I feel like an explorer, discovering something new each time.

Outside the historic area, this city has some great places to run along the beach, through residential neighborhoods, and at nearby state parks. In addition, some of Northeast Florida's most popular races are held in St. Augustine.

BEST PLACES TO RUN

Anastasia State Recreation Area: A favorite spot of local runners, this is a great place to do a relaxed run along the Atlantic Ocean, especially since cars are no longer allowed to drive on the beach. Located along A1A in St. Augustine Beach, the park is open year round. The main entrance is off A1A and Anastasia Park Road, right past the St. Augustine Lighthouse. An admission fee is required at this entrance. Another way to get on the beach is to enter the park from the south side. There is no admission fee and the entrance is on A1A Beach Boulevard and Pope Road. There is a small public parking lot next to the Howard Johnson Motel on the north side of A1A Beach Boulevard. There is a short ramp that takes you right into Anastasia State Recreation Area beach. From this point it is three miles to the inlet so you can get a nice six-mile run on the beach if you go all the way and back. There are more people in the evening, so if you prefer solitude it is better to run in the morning. For more information call the park staff at: (904) 461-2033 or visit www.dep.state.fl.us/parks/district3/anastasia.

Bridge of Lions: Rising above the Matanzas River, the Bridge of Lions is one of St. Augustine's most beautiful sights. The bridge con-

The legendary Bridge of Lions in St. Augustine

nects the historic center with residential areas on Anastasia Island. Every July this is the course of one of the most popular 5K races in North Florida. Start by the main entrance of the Castillo de San Marcos, the impressive seventeenth century Spanish fort, and run south on Avenida Menendez towards the Bridge of Lions. Stay on the sidewalk closest to the river. Turn left to go over the bridge and keep to the left sidewalk. As soon as you cross the bridge, make a left on North St. Augustine Boulevard. Here you will be in the Davis Shores neighborhood, a beautiful residential area with no sidewalks. Continue on North St. Augustine Boulevard. The road will swerve around and eventually become Inlet Drive. Stay on Inlet Drive until it changes into Comares Avenue. Keep running on this street until you get to Flagler Boulevard. Make a right on Flagler Boulevard and keep going for a couple of blocks until Arredondo Avenue. Make a right and stay on Arredondo Avenue until you reach North St. Augustine Boulevard. Make a left and this will take you back to the Bridge of Lions. Veer to the right as you approach the bridge. Continue over the bridge towards the Castillo de San Marcos where you started. This loop is about 3.6 miles.

Guana River State Park: This natural preserve is located on A1A about seven miles north of Vilano Beach. The park is located between the Atlantic Ocean and the Intracoastal Waterway. There are several entrances, but the trail area is located at the southernmost section of the park along the west side of A1A. Follow the signs into the park. There is a small admission fee. Here you will see the Guana Dam area. Parking is available here. The trails start across the small dam behind the wooden post. There are several color-coded trails totaling about nine miles. There is a map available by the entrance of the trail area. This is a great place if you enjoy trail running. The area is mostly flat and swampy with very diverse wildlife. The trails are soft and padded with leaves. Bring water along and wear insect repellent. The park is open from 8:00 A.M. until sundown. Just in case trails are not your thing, the park has several miles of beaches across the street from A1A. The beach is pristine and beautiful. There are three parking areas along A1A north of the trail area. Keep in mind that these are protected areas so try to leave only footprints behind. For more information contact the Guana River State Park at: (904) 825-5071 or visit www.dep.state.fl.us/parks/district3/guanariver.

Historic District: The historic area of St. Augustine extends through several blocks and is usually full of activity and tourists. Because the streets are very old and narrow most don't have side-walks, and although a big section of St. George Street is closed to vehicles, many streets allow one way traffic. Most intersections have four-way stop signs which make traffic slow but still dangerous for runners. It is best to avoid the tourist area during peak hours and always run with extra care. Here's a loop around the perimeter of the historic district that gives a sense of the historic area while helping you avoid the most congested streets: Start on West Castillo Drive near the Visitor Information Center and run towards San Marco Avenue. Make a right on San Marco Avenue and continue south. Right in front of the Visitor Information Center, San Marco Avenue becomes Castillo Drive. Keep going and a block away you will see the Castillo de San Marcos to your left. Right past the fort, the street changes to Avenida Menendez. Try to run on the right-hand side-walk. Continue straight on Avenida Menendez. You will be running parallel to the Matanzas River/Intracoastal Waterway, and you will pass by several historic inns, restaurants, and the main square. This area can be congested sometimes, so watch for pedestrians and traf-fic. About eight blocks from the Castillo you will get to St. Francis Street. Make a right on St. Francis and keep going until Cordova

Waterfront Avenida Menendez, St. Augustine

Street. Make a right on Cordova Street and continue a long block until Bridge Street. Make a left on Bridge Street by the Firehouse. Go one block and make a right on Granada Street. Go straight until it ends on King Street. Here you will be in front of Flagler College's main building. Make a left on King Street and turn right half a block away on Sevilla Street. Stay on this street until it ends on Valencia Street and make a left. Go a block and a half and turn right on Riberia Street. Stay on Riberia Street for several blocks until you come to West Castillo Drive. Make a right and you will be by the baseball fields. Keep going until you see the Visitor Information Center area where you started. This loop is 2.5 miles.

Lighthouse Area: The red, black, and white St. Augustine Lighthouse is located off Anastasia Boulevard (A1A) about a mile from the Bridge of Lions and downtown area. You will see the lighthouse from the road. There is a small parking lot in front of the main entrance. From here you can run through several residential neighborhoods around the lighthouse and nearby Anastasia State Recreation Area. Most streets don't have sidewalks, so watch for cars.

St. Augustine Beach: Just south of Anastasia State Park is St.

17

Augustine Beach. Run on A1A Beach Boulevard which goes parallel to the ocean for approximately two miles past hotels, shops, and condominiums. There is parking at the south end of this road at Anastasia Plaza Shopping Center. Park here and run north on A1A Beach Boulevard. There are sidewalks on both sides of the street. If you want to increase the mileage, turn into any of the streets west of A1A Beach Boulevard. Here you will find plenty of well-shaded residential streets to run on.

BEST LOCAL RACES

Matanzas 5K: This race is held during the last weekend in January. It is perhaps the largest and most popular 5K in Northeast Florida. The race starts on Castillo Drive by the baseball fields and goes through the historic section of the city. The course is flat with lots of turns on narrow streets. A free one-mile fun run for kids is held after the main event, where the first several hundred finishers receive a tee-shirt and a ribbon. The post-race celebration is one of the best I know of. Every year hundreds of dollars in expensive prizes such as watches, bikes, TVs, running gear, and gift certificates are given away. This is a great event to include on your list. For me this race signals the beginning of a new running year. Plus, the winter weather in North Florida is great for running.

Twilight Lighthouse 5K: This traditional 5K is held in mid-March at the St. Augustine Lighthouse. The course is flat and fast, providing an excellent chance for a PR (personal record). The race is in the late afternoon and starts/finishes in front of the lighthouse museum building. There is a free one-mile fun run held right after the 5K event. The post-race party is great with good food, sport drinks, free beer and live music. If you have never been to the St. Augustine Lighthouse this is a great occasion. All runners get to climb the 219 steps to the top of the lighthouse at no charge. The view of the city is awesome. I enjoy this afternoon race because it is fast, and it gives me a good reason to visit lovely St. Augustine, which is always even more beautiful in the evening.

Gamble Rogers Folk Festival 10K: This 10K is held in the early afternoon in May as part of the Gamble Rogers Folk Festival. The race starts by the R.B. Hunt Elementary School near the St. Augustine Lighthouse and finishes by the St. Augustine Amphitheatre. The course goes through several residential streets and part of Anastasia State Park including a trail section. If you are looking for a small event in a beautiful setting, try this one.

Bridge of Lions 5K: This popular evening event is held in mid-July. The race starts by the historic Castillo de San Marcos and goes over the Bridge of Lions continuing through residential streets to finish back at the bridge. Except for the bridge, the course is flat and fast. Almost a thousand runners enter this 5K every year making it one of the largest in the area. The post-race party starts at the finish area and then moves across the bridge to the Old Market Square for the awards ceremony. This race is always high on my list. It has a special attraction that keeps me coming back year after year. Perhaps it is the feeling of being amidst all that history, sharing the warm summer evening with hundreds of runners, or perhaps it is because it reminds me of where I started long ago as a runner. This is definitely a great race.

RUNNING CLUBS

Ancient City Road Runners (ACRR): Based in St. Augustine, this is a very active and well-organized running club. Several weekly training group runs are available. A membership fee is required to join. For more information write to: ACRR, P.O. Box 4111, St. Augustine, FL, 32085-4111, or visit www.ancientcityrr.org.

OTHER RESOURCES

City of St. Augustine Official Website: Here you will find a wealth of information about St. Augustine such as local weather, calendar of events, etc. www.ci.st-augustine.fl.us.

City of St. Augustine Beach Official Website: This site contains lots of practical information about St. Augustine Beach. www.staug-bch.com.

St. Augustine Visitors and Convention Bureau: This site contains lots of useful information about this area. www.visitoldcity.com.

The St. Augustine Record Online: Here you will find the latest news and information about St. Augustine. www.staugustine.com.

PALATKA AREA

Palatka, the bass fishing capital of the world, is located in Putnam County where US 17 crosses the St. Johns River. This picturesque city is less than one hour from Jacksonville, Gainesville, and St. Augustine. Here you will find an old-time business district, several blocks of historic homes and a couple of great places to run that are worth the drive. After the run make sure to visit Angels Dining Car, a local landmark since 1932, located in the center of town on US 17 (Reid Street) between 2nd and 3rd streets. The food is great and quite inexpensive.

BEST PLACES TO RUN

Ravine Gardens State Park: The Ravine Gardens is located on Twigg Street near the St. Johns River, only one block south of South 15th Street and River Street. The park has a steep ravine surrounded by beautiful Florida vegetation. There is a shaded 1.8-mile paved road that loops around the park and several walking trails leading down into the ravine. The area is very scenic and makes you feel far away from civilization. This is an excellent place to do hill training in a relaxed, natural setting. The 1.8-mile loop makes it easy to meet your distance needs by running once, twice, or as many times you want around the park. This is one of my favorite Florida state parks to run in. The park is well maintained and unique. Running this place is a must if you visit the area. Restrooms, water, and picnic tables are found by the main entrance behind the parking lot. There is a small admission fee. Bring the family along and let them walk through the azalea gardens while you run the loop. The park is open from 8:00 A.M. until sundown. For more information call the park at (904) 329-3721 or visit www.dep.state.fl.us/parks/district3/ravinegardens/

River Street Historic Area: This is one of Palatka's most scenic historic neighborhoods. The area is reminiscent of a period of time several decades past. Here you can run through beautiful residential streets surrounded by historic homes, many dating back to the nineteenth century. Most of the streets are shaded and have sidewalks. Watch for traffic at crossings. For a nice run, start in front of the City

Dock parking lot located on River Street and Laurel Street, and run south along River Street. You will be running parallel to the St. Johns River until the road goes over the railroad tracks, gets hilly, and veers right to end on South 15th Street. At this point you will have completed a mile. Turn right on South 15th Street and continue straight until Kirby Street. Turn right on Kirby Street and keep going straight. You will pass the railroad tracks as well as some factories and a cemetery on the left side. Continue on Kirby Street until Laurel Street. Turn right on Laurel Street and keep going until you see River Street and the City Dock parking area where you started. This loop is two miles total. There is parking available by the City Dock area. For a more intense workout, run from the City Dock parking lot to the other side of the Memorial Bridge and back. Run on the road parallel to the river. The Memorial Bridge is very steep and about two thirds of a mile long. When running on the bridge use the pedestrian sidewalk. This loop is about two miles.

BEST LOCAL RACES

Catfish 5K: This race is the kickoff event of the famous Catfish Festival held every April in Crescent City. This old-fashioned

A hill workout, Memorial Bridge, US 17, Palatka

Victorian style town is located twenty miles south of Palatka on US 17. The 5K race starts on US 17 (Summit Street) in the center of town and goes through several shaded streets along the banks of Lake Crescent to finish back at the starting area. Although the course is mostly flat and fast, some parts have rolling hills and steep grades. The post-race awards ceremony is held right across from the Catfish Festival area. The festival activities include live music, craft exhibits, great food, and a colorful parade. The combination of the 5K run and festival makes this a great family event. One year I ran this race, my whole family came with me, and after the parade we ate brunch at The Coffee Shop, an old-fashioned place located on Summit Street and Florida Avenue. The food was great and the atmosphere was really like being in the 50s. Everybody had a good time.

Floyd 4M: This event is held in May during Palatka's Blue Crab Festival weekend. The four-mile race has become a Northeast Florida tradition attracting several hundred runners every year. The certified course is very challenging and scenic. The race begins on River Street and goes through the Ravine Gardens State Park and back. After the hard run there is plenty of food, prizes and the opportunity to mingle with local runners at the post-race party. In addition, the famous Blue Crab Festival is held only a couple of blocks from the race area in the center of town. Here you will find crafts, live music, great food, and plenty of activities for the whole family. I ran this race a couple of years ago and loved the views at the Ravine Gardens. True to its claim, I found the course challenging, and although the first mile was uphill, the last was downhill and fast. After the awards party, we checked out the music and food at the nearby Blue Crab Festival. If you are looking for a well-organized event, a picturesque festival, and a unique course, try the Floyd four-miler next May.

RUNNING CLUBS

Putnam Runners Club: After over a decade of actively sponsoring running events, this Palatka club folded in early 2001. The main reason was the low number of members in recent years. Along with the club two popular local races ended their long traditions: the Mug Run 5K and the Johnny Branam Memorial 2M. But not all is lost. There are still many active runners in this community, and a few remaining local events have been picked up by neighboring running clubs. For the latest information about the Putnam Runners Club, visit the RRCA Florida club website at www.rrca.org.

OTHER RESOURCES

Palatka Daily News Online: Here you can get the latest local happenings. www.palatkadailynews.com.

Putnam County Chamber of Commerce Official Website: It contains a wealth of information for visitors, such as a calendar of events and lodging directory. www.putnamcountychamber.org.

Putnam County Community and Tourism Official Website: There is lots of useful information about the community. www.putnamcountyfl.com.

 ## GAINESVILLE AREA

Home to the University of Florida and the famous Gators football team, this historic college town is considered by many to be the Eugene, Oregon of the East, a training mecca for elite distance runners during the winter months. Here they find low cost of living, excellent coaching, and a wide range of running options in a world-class atmosphere. Many of the best European and American long distance runners have been coming to Gainesville year after year since the early 1970s. Olympians Jack Bacheler, Frank Shorter, and Grete Waitz are just a few of the top-notch runners that have trained in Gainesville.

Today, Gainesville enjoys one of the highest concentrations of runners per capita in the country. This is no surprise in a progressive city with so many running options. There are dozens of places to run, including miles of shaded city streets, suburban residential areas, pristine nature trails, and the huge University of Florida campus. Although most of Florida is low and flat, several areas in this city are quite hilly, giving runners an even greater training diversity.

Over the years Gainesville has become one of my favorite places to run in North Florida. Running here, I always feel inspired by the beautiful surroundings and energized by the college atmosphere.

BEST PLACES TO RUN

Gainesville to Hawthorne Rail Trail: The trailhead is accessible in Gainesville at Boulware Springs City Park, which is located on 3300 SE 15th Street two miles south of East University Avenue and about four miles from the main University of Florida Campus. Parking is available at Boulware Springs Park and near the trailhead entrance area. The park has restrooms, water, picnic tables and emergency phones. Once in the trail, there are restrooms at mile 1 and mile 6.6. Bring water along. Maps are available by the trailhead entrance area. The trail is about ten feet wide; it is paved and has mile markers. It goes for almost sixteen miles through Paynes Prairie and the Lochloosa Wildlife Management area ending in the town of Hawthorne. The trail was built over part of an old railroad line. This is a very scenic and inviting trail surrounded with beautiful trees and colorful meadows. Many bicyclists, hikers, and roller skaters use this

Boulware Springs trailhead, start of the Gainesville-Hawthorne State Trail

trail, so run with caution. There is also a parallel horse trail. A great place to run in a natural and secluded setting, the trail is open from 8 A.M. until sundown. For more information call the park staff at (352) 466-3397 or visit www.dep.state.fl.us/parks/district2/gainesville-hawthorne.

NW 34th Street: Start at the southeast corner of NW 34th Street and NW 8th Avenue, across from Westside Park. Head south on NW 34th Street towards West University Avenue. Run on the left sidewalk. As you get closer to West University Avenue you will see more commerce. Turn left on West University Avenue, and continue straight towards the UF Campus. When you get to NW 22nd Street turn left. This is right before the campus stadium area. Continue on NW 22nd Street. The sidewalk is on the right side. Turn left on NW 8th Avenue, and keep going until NW 34th Street where you started. This loop is 3.3 miles.

Great unpaved nature trails at San Felasco Hammock, Gainesville

NW 43rd Street: Starting on NW 43rd Street and NW 8th Avenue, run north on 43rd Street. This street has sidewalks on both sides and goes for several miles in a straight line. The sidewalk ends around NW 53rd Avenue. The course is flat and easy. Stay on the sidewalk and watch for cars when crossing intersections.

San Felasco Hammock State Preserve: This beautiful nature trail area is located on SR 232, about 3.5 miles west of the Devil's Millhopper Geological site (NW 53rd Avenue). There is a small parking lot on the left if you are driving west on SR 232. The preserve's entrance is a few hundred yards east of I-75. There is an admission fee per car. Leave the receipt stub visible on your dashboard. There are two picnic tables and a bathroom behind the parking area. Bring water since there isn't any available. The park has three main trails totaling more than eleven miles. The shortest trail, about a mile long, starts behind the parking lot. The other two trails start across the road from the parking area. These are much longer, about 4.9 and 5.6 miles, and have color markers on the trees. The terrain is soft and sometimes hilly, meandering through pine forests, maples, and a myriad of Florida vegetation. The park is very big. You may want to run with a friend and stick to the marked trails, especially if you are unfamiliar with the area. Dogs are allowed on a leash. Wear insect repellent to avoid mosquitoes and other flying insects. This park is one of the preferred spots for local and elite runners. Many of them run here on weekends. The park is open every day from 8 A.M. until sundown. For more information call the San Felasco Hammock State Preserve at (352) 955-2008 or visit www.dep.state.fl.us/parks/district2/sanfelasco.

University of Florida Campus: This is a very large campus which covers several blocks of green areas, gothic-style buildings, and shaded streets. Located between West University Avenue, SW 13th Street, Archer Road, and SW 34th Street, the campus' perimeter is about five miles. The UF campus is a great place to log several miles in a relaxed college atmosphere. The area around Museum Road is very scenic and a favorite spot among college runners. Most streets have sidewalks and a bike lane. Restrooms are available throughout the campus and at the track. For an area map visit www.ufl.edu/visitors.html, or stop by the Office of Admissions on weekdays between 10 A.M. and 2 P.M.

Westside Park: This centrally located city park is popular with local runners. The main entrance is on NW 34th Street across from Littlewood Elementary School, which is less than half a block from NW 8th Avenue. The park has free parking, playgrounds, picnic tables, tennis courts, restrooms, and grass fields. Although the park perimeter is not much longer than a mile, this is a great place to use as base point to park and go for a run into the surrounding areas. Several races held here use the park as start and finish points while the main course wanders through the shaded and steep adjacent streets. For a great run, start on NW 34th Street by the parking lot and run north towards NW 16th Avenue. Use the sidewalk. Turn right on NW 16th Avenue, and keep going straight. There will be a long steep stretch ahead. Keep going until NW 22nd Street. Turn right on NW 22nd Street. The sidewalk is on the eastern side of the street. Keep going straight for about half a mile until NW 8th Avenue. Turn right on NW 8th Avenue and stay on the right-side sidewalk. There will be a long downhill stretch (this is my favorite part). Keep going straight. As you get closer to the park you will go by NW 31st Drive and see the beginning of the park grounds on your right. Continue running on NW 8th Avenue until NW 34th Street, which is only a few hundred yards away. Turn right on NW 34th Street, and keep going until you reach the parking area where you started. This loop is 3.4 miles.

BEST LOCAL RACES

Greater Gainesville 5K: Held in February, this is Gainesville's most popular running event. The race starts and finishes in the downtown area and goes through historic neighborhoods. This 5K event attracts hundreds of runners including elite level competitors training in the area. This race is definitely a must if you find yourself in Gainesville in February.

Haile Plantation Tri-State Run: This race is held in April. There are three events that start together: a 5K, a 10K, and a 15K. The course is a fast and almost flat 5K loop, so depending on which distance you enter you go once, twice or three times around. The races start and finish in the center of town in the Haile Plantation development. A few years ago I ran the 5K race and really enjoyed both the fast course and the post-race party. There was something for everyone. This is a great course to attempt a PR time in one of these distances.

Melon Run 3M: This picturesque race is held on the Fourth of July every year since 1979. This popular three-miler starts and finishes at Westside Park. The course has a steep stretch but ends downhill. There is a one-mile fun run for kids after the main event. If you are in Gainesville around Independence Day this is a great way to celebrate our freedom.

Dog Days Run: This traditional event is held in September at Westside Park. It consists of two races: a 5K and a one-mile fun run for dogs and their owners. Both events start and finish at the park. The 5K course goes out and back through the surrounding residential streets. This event is a must if you have a canine friend. There is even a special awards category for them.

Micanopy Half-Marathon: This race is held in October in Micanopy, a small town located ten miles south of Gainesville. This event consists of two races: the half-marathon and a 5K. The race starts in the center of town and goes through some hilly surrounding areas. This is a wonderful opportunity to see the scenic fall foliage of North Central Florida.

RUNNING CLUBS

Florida Track Club: The FTC is the largest and oldest running club in Gainesville. Open to all people, this is a very active group and a great place to meet local runners. A membership fee is required to join. For more information call (352) 378-8725 or write to: FTC, P.O. Box 12463, Gainesville, FL, 32604. www.floridatrackclub.org.

Gainesville Front Runners: This is the local chapter of the International Front Runners organization, a group of gay/lesbian/bisexual runners and walkers. The club is open to everyone. www.afn.org/~frunners/main.html.

OTHER RESOURCES

Alachua County Visitors and Convention Bureau: Located at 30 East University Avenue in Gainesville, the Bureau offers great information about Gainesville and surrounding areas. Call them at (352)

374-5231 or (352) 333-2520 (weekends), or visit www.visit-gainesville.net.

City of Gainesville Official Website: It contains lots of information and links. www.cityofgainesville.org.

Lloyd Clarke Sports: This store is a big sponsor of local races and a supporter of the Gainesville running community. Although it is not a specialty running store, it carries a large selection of running shoes and running gear. Lloyd Clarke Sports is located about a mile north of the main UF campus at 1504 NW 13th Street. Telephone: (352) 372-7836. www.lloydclarkesports.com.

Run Florida: This is a specialty store dedicated to meeting the needs of the Gainesville running community. It is a good place to get information about upcoming races. The store hosts weekly runs in the area. Run Florida is located across the street from the main UF campus at 1702 West University Avenue (352) 271-0268. www.run-florida.com.

The Gainesville Sun **Online:** offers the latest local news and events www.gainesvillesun.com.

 **TALLAHASSEE AREA**

Situated among low rolling hills halfway between Jacksonville and Pensacola, this charming city is both Florida's capital and a big college town. Tallahassee has many places to run such as parks, college campuses, a beautiful and safe downtown, some of the best trails in Florida, and shaded roads in picturesque neighborhoods. Most streets have sidewalks and there are many hilly areas for a great workout. The local running community is well organized and active, hosting several running events throughout the year. In short, Tallahassee is a runner-friendly city with something for everyone.

BEST PLACES TO RUN

Capitol Area: Downtown Tallahassee is a beautiful area. The streets have sidewalks and are well maintained. For a scenic run around the State's Capitol area start on Monroe Street and Park Avenue by the small city park area. This is about two blocks north of the Capitol buildings. Head north on Monroe Street towards Tennessee Street. Use the sidewalk on the west side. Turn left on Tennessee Street and continue for about three blocks until Bronough Street. Make a left and stay on Bronough Street until Madison Street. Turn left on Madison Street and keep going until you get to Monroe Street. The Capitol buildings will be on your left. Make a left on Monroe Street and you will pass in front of the old Capitol building. Continue on Monroe Street towards Park Avenue where you started. This loop is 1.6 miles. There is metered parking on Park Avenue and Monroe Street along the park area. Watch for traffic at intersections. It is best to avoid running during peak business hours.

Florida State University Campus: This large gothic-style campus is located in downtown Tallahassee just a few blocks west of the State Capitol area between M. L. King Jr. Boulevard, Tennessee Street, Stadium Drive, and Gaines Street. Within this perimeter you will find over one hundred buildings along shaded streets with live oaks, several rolling hills, and beautiful green areas. For a short but scenic run start by Bill's Bookstore on Copeland Street and Park Avenue. Head north on Copeland Street until Call Street. Make a left on Call Street. Continue straight until Dogwood Way. Make a left on Dogwood Way. Continue straight until Florida Drive. Turn right on Florida Drive and then left on Jefferson Street. Continue straight until Copeland Street. Make a left on Copeland Street and keep going until Park Avenue where you started. This loop is 1.2 miles. For a slightly longer loop start by Bill's Bookstore and head north on Copeland Street until Tennessee Street. Make a left on Tennessee Street and continue straight. This area has more traffic, so be cautious and use the sidewalk. Make a left on Woodward Avenue and stay on this until Jefferson Street. Make a left on Jefferson Street. Continue on Jefferson Street until you see Copeland Street. Make a left on Copeland Street and Park Avenue is just two blocks away. This loop is 1.7 miles. Most streets have sidewalks. Restrooms and water are available throughout the campus area. If you are looking for a relaxed run in a beautiful college setting give this a try. Campus runs are among my favorites. For a map, see www.fsu.edu/Campus/newmap.

Lake Overstreet Area: The Lake Overstreet area is part of the Alfred B. Maclay State Gardens. Here you will find some excellent multi-use trails around the lake and surrounding woods. A convenient place to find parking near the trailhead area is in the Forestmeadows Park & Athletic Center at 4750 North Meridian Road. This is a city tennis and fitness center located on the west side of the street just under a mile north of Maclay Road. Water and restrooms are available at the Forestmeadows building. The Lake Overstreet trail access is right across the road from the entrance to the Forestmeadows center. You will see posted signs leading to the trail entrance. Watch out for incoming traffic when crossing Meridian Road. There are maps and trail signs at the trailhead entrance. There is a small fee, honor system. From this point you can run in either direction of the trail since this will eventually loop around to where you started. The figure-8 main trail is about five miles long with basically two loops connected by a hilly stretch. The trail is very wooded and scenic. Bring water and wear bug repellent.

Watch for bikes, tree roots, and wildlife. This is one of the locals' favorite trails. The trail is open daily from 8 A.M. until sundown.

Miller Landing Area: This area is located on Miller Landing Road about a block north of the Forestmeadows Park & Athletic Center. From Meridian Road turn left on Miller Landing Road and

Miller Landing Trail, Tallahassee

31

the Meadows Soccer Complex entrance is a third of a mile on your left. The Red Bug Trail and the Meadows Soccer Complex area are both part of the Elinor Klapp – Phipps Park. The Forestmeadows center is right in between these. Here you will find plenty of parking as well as access to several multi-use dirt trails. The trail area is located just west of the parking lot. Follow the signs pointing to the trail access. The trails are marked and they total several miles across woods and scenic rolling hills. Lake Jackson is located west of the park. Keep in mind that these trails are shared with bikers, horses, and hikers, so be mindful of them. Bring water, wear bug repellent, and watch for wildlife. The trail area is open daily from sunrise to sunset.

Park Avenue Loop: Park Avenue is a charming street lined with beautiful homes, live oaks, and shaded sidewalks reminiscent of the

Run through historic residential areas, Park Avenue, Tallahassee.

old south. The road goes east to west through downtown ending at Florida State University. For a scenic run through this historic area, start from the Magnolia Park Courtyard shopping plaza on Park Avenue and Magnolia Drive. This is also the Winn Dixie shopping center. Here you will find plenty of parking, food, and restrooms. Head west on Park Avenue, but be careful crossing the intersection. Run on the left side sidewalk. Continue on Park Avenue towards the center of town. The road will get hilly for a while but keep going. Stay on Park Avenue and go past Monroe Street. A few blocks ahead you will see the Old City Cemetery on your right between M. L. King Jr. Street and Macomb Street. Continue one more block and Park Avenue will end on Copeland Street. You will see Bill's Bookstore on your left at the corner of Copeland Street and Park Avenue. From this point turn around and head back to Magnolia Drive. This loop is 3.8 miles. For a longer run increase the mileage with one of the loops around the FSU campus (see above).

Red Bug Trail: The Red Bug Trail is part of the Elinor Klapp – Phipps Park. The trail begins at the south end of the Forestmeadows Park & Athletic Center. Walk past the parking lot and tennis courts and you will see the trailhead. There is a trail map with information by the entrance. This is a narrow wooded multi-use trail with lots of wildlife, turns, rolling hills, tree roots, and wet areas. The trail is very tough and about three miles long. Many mountain bikers use the trail, so be cautious at all times. Bring water and wear bug repellent. Parking and restrooms are available at the Forestmeadows center located at 4750 North Meridian Road, a little north of Maclay Road. If you enjoy challenges, try this trail. Many local runners including the FSU cross-country team train here.

San Luis Mission Park: This is a beautiful wooded park maintained by the City of Tallahassee. The area is very shaded and sort of hidden. The park has free parking, restrooms, water, picnic tables, and a playground. An area map can be found outside the restroom facilities. There is a 1.8-mile trail loop around the park. The trail goes through woods, over several hills, and crosses over a long wooden bridge by Lake Esther. This is a popular training spot among local trail runners including FSU's cross-country team. This is a great place for trail running and a good hill workout. If you decide to try it, watch for tree roots and wear bug repellent. San Luis Park is open daily from sunrise to sunset. The main entrance is located off San Luis Road. Take Ocala Road to Tharpe Street. Make a left on Tharpe Street and continue west for less than half a mile until you see San Luis Road. Make a left on San Luis Road, and the entrance to the park should be about a third of a mile down on the left side. Follow the signs into the park. For longer runs, an option is to do several loops around the trail or combine this with a run through the park's adjacent streets. San Luis Road is quite hilly and has a long sidewalk.

Tallahassee-St. Marks Trail: Built over an old railroad line, this was Florida's first official state trail. The St. Marks Trail is one of the most popular places to run in the Capital City. The asphalt path is about eight feet wide and goes for sixteen miles parallel to SR 363 from Tallahassee to the town of St. Marks on the Gulf Coast. The trail is located about 4.7 miles south of Gaines Street and Monroe Street, near the Capitol building. Take Monroe Street (Road 61), and head south until Woodville Highway (SR 363). Continue on Woodville Highway past Capital Circle. The trail entrance is on the right side about a quarter of a mile after Capital Circle. Here you will find free parking, a bike rental store, picnic tables, a water fountain, and restrooms. There is also a horse trail parallel to the paved path. The scenic trail is mainly flat, tree-lined, and crosses forests, wildlife refuges, and several small roads. Many bikers, hikers and roller skaters also use this trail so run with caution and bring water if you decide to go for a long run. The trail is open from 8 A.M. until sundown. For more information call (850) 922-6007 or visit www.dep.state.fl.us/parks/district1/stmarkstrail.

Thomasville Road Loop: A very popular place to run is the area around Thomasville Road. This is a beautiful residential neighborhood with shaded streets and some rolling hills. A convenient place to start your run is the Capital Plaza shopping center located on Thomasville Road about a half-block before Glenview Road. Here you will find plenty of parking and several retail stores. Thomasville Road is a busy road with sidewalks on both sides. From the shopping plaza head north on Thomasville Road past the BP gas station. Stay on Thomasville Road until you get to Armistead Road. Turn right on Armistead Road. This is a quiet street with no sidewalk, so use caution. Continue for about a mile and turn right into Marston Place.

Here the road gets narrow and winds around under a canopy of trees. This is a dead end street that ends at a cul-de-sac. Go around the circle and head back to the shopping center the same way you came. This loop is about 4.4 miles. For a longer run there are many side streets along Armistead Road and Thomasville Road. Also, a local running group meets early Sunday mornings at the BP gas station for a run in the area.

Tom Brown Park: This is a large city park located off Capitol Circle behind the Federal Correctional Institute (FCI). From Capitol Circle turn east into Easterwood Drive by the National Guard Armory and follow the signs to the park. The entrance will be on your left. The park has several multi-purpose facilities, a BMX track, picnic tables, and a service road around the open grass fields. In addition, here you will find some of the best trails in Leon County. The park has several interconnected trails. The Magnolia trail starts behind the BMX track. Other trails can be accessed near the picnic area. Most are shaded and some are quite hilly. This is a great place to do your off-the-road hill workouts. Several local runners and high school teams train here. If you decide to run these trails watch for tree roots, mountain bikers, hikers, and wildlife. Bring water and wear insect repellent. If trails are not your thing, the park has several paved roads that can add up to a few miles if you run them back and forth. Also, the Lincoln High School track is located across the street from the southernmost end of the park. Here you can boost your run with a few speed intervals. Restrooms, water, and free parking are available at the park. The park is open daily from sunrise to sunset.

BEST LOCAL RACES

Tallahassee Marathon: The Tallahassee Marathon is held in the second half of January. The event consists of three races: the marathon, a half-marathon, and a two-mile fun run. All races start and finish at the Tallahassee Nurseries on Thomasville Road, but the marathon and half-marathon begin earlier. The course is mostly shaded and passes through several residential areas northeast of downtown. The area is beautiful and there are some rolling hills. The post race party is much fun with food, drinks, and entertainment for everyone. Although this is not a big marathon it has been held continuously for over two decades, and every year more than a hundred runners return determined to keep the tradition alive. If you are looking for a memorable marathon but want to avoid the large crowds of bigger events, try this one. Plus, the January weather in northwest Florida is made for running.

Flash 12K: This event is held in February. The 12K run starts in front of Chaires Elementary School and continues through beautiful country roads and several rolling hills to finish near the starting area under a big oak tree. The post-race celebration offers lots of fun for everyone, awards for each age group, and pies for the winners. The Flash run is an unusual event, not just because 12K is a rarer distance, but because the race got its name from a popular comic book, and its tee-shirts have featured the Flash theme since the beginning. Every year more than a hundred runners take part in this unique experience. This is a great opportunity to run one of the few 12Ks held in Florida and the chance to get one of the prized Flash tee-shirts. Chaires Elementary School is located east of downtown on Chaires Cross Road.

Springtime 10K: This race is held in late March in downtown as part of the Springtime Tallahassee Festival. The Springtime 10K is Tallahassee's biggest running event. Every year almost a thousand runners gather at the starting line. The race starts in front of the Leon County Courthouse on Monroe Street. The course goes downhill the first mile and then through rolling hills through the Myers Park neighborhood, one of the prettiest areas in the city. The finish area is in front of the FDOT building on Suwannee Street. In addition to the 10K, there is a one-mile run for those under seventeen years old that begins right after the main run. Its course is mostly downhill, starting and finishing at the same locations as the 10K. The awards party is held near the finish area. Here you will find lots of food and refreshments, but the celebration continues after the awards ceremony. There is a colorful street parade, crafts, food, music, and kids' activities throughout the area. The Springtime 10K is a great event for the whole family; you get to run, and everybody gets to enjoy the festivities following the race.

Palace Saloon 5K: This 5K run is held in April. The race starts at James Messer Field located on Jackson Bluff Road across from the

Florida Highway Patrol Academy. This is a very popular event and perhaps the oldest race in Tallahassee. It was held for the first time in 1975 and today it is still going strong. Following the run there is a great post-race celebration with lots of food, refreshments, and fun for everyone. If you are looking for an all-around memorable event, try the Palace Saloon 5K.

Tom Brown Bash: This traditional cross-country event is held in late August at Tom Brown Park. There are two races: the five-mile "bash" and a three-mile run. Both events start and finish near the large pavilion inside the park. The course is mostly off-road through trails that have plenty of hills and obstacles. In fact, the combination of heat, humidity, and difficult terrain can make this race a tough challenge even for the best athletes. Perhaps this is what has made this run so popular. Each year over two hundred runners show up for this unique experience. If you are looking for a great race to test your endurance or just want to try a true cross-country event, consider this one. Tom Brown Park is located off of Capital Circle about 500 feet south of E. Park Avenue in Tallahassee.

Run for Sickle Cell: This popular event is held in September to benefit the Sickle Cell Foundation. There are two races: a 5K and a one-mile fun run. The 5K race starts and finishes at the Jake Gaither Recreation Center & Golf Course located on Tanner Drive just a few blocks southwest of the FAMU campus. The course is mostly flat and fast through the surrounding streets. The awards ceremony has plenty of food, refreshments, and music. This race has been around for many years. It is a well-organized event and one worth considering. Every year over two hundred runners come out to show their support and have a good time.

Women's Distance Festival: This run is held in October at Optimist Park. There are actually three races: a 5K for women, a 5K for men, and a one-mile fun run. The women's 5K starts first, and it is the main event. This race is part of the RRCA national women's distance running series which started in 1980 as a way to promote women's distance races around the country. The goal is to get people to participate, especially women, regardless of their fitness level. There is a fun post-race party with food, refreshments, and lots of prize drawings. Proceeds from the event go to charity. Optimist Park is located at 1800 East Indianhead Drive. Parking and restroom facilities are available at Hartsfield Elementary School located on Chowkeebin Nene street, only a couple of blocks from the starting area. This is a great race to show support for our fellow runners.

Turkey Trot Run: This traditional event is held in November on Thanksgiving Day. It consists of three races: a 5K, a 10K, and a 15K. The Turkey Trot has been one of Tallahassee's running traditions. It started in 1978 and in the 1980s it went through many changes in date, location, and course distance. But the Turkey Trot survived, and today it attracts several hundred runners every year. All three runs start and finish on Tram Road near the Leon County Fairgrounds. The course is mostly flat and loops through the surrounding streets. There is also a one-mile fun run for kids before the main event. The post-race party is staged at the Leon County Fairgrounds, and there is plenty of food and refreshments for everyone. Whether you run the 5K, 10K, or 15K, this is a great chance to burn some extra calories while supporting a good cause in the spirit of Thanksgiving. Part of the event's proceeds are donated to a local shelter. If you find yourself in Tallahassee this time of year, make this race part of your Thanksgiving tradition.

Jingle Bell Run: This popular 3K run is held in December. This evening event is part of the Winter Festival Celebration of Lights in downtown Tallahassee. The race starts on Monroe Street and Call Street and loops through the business and government district to finish back at the starting area. This is a very unique race which attracts hundreds of runners every year. Many runners wear Santa hats and jingle bells on their shoes. The starting of the race is a spectacle in itself with the sound of thousands of jingling bells as runners move forward. After the race the celebration continues with a holiday parade and live entertainment. This is a fun family event and a chance to share with others in the spirit of the holidays, especially since runners are asked to bring a new toy as part of their registration. These toys are donated to local children's organizations. If you are looking for something fun and unique in December, come out and join the jingle bells.

RUNNING CLUBS

Gulf Winds Track Club: Started in the early 1970s, the GWTC is among the largest and best organized running clubs in Florida today. Open to everyone, the club offers weekly training groups and social events, and it sponsors several popular races throughout the year. In addition, the GWTC has one of the most complete running websites, offering information about the local running such as calendar of events, training tips, group run schedules, news, and links. A membership fee is required to join. For more information, write to: GWTC, P.O. Box 3447, Tallahassee, FL, 32315, or visit www.gulfwinds.org.

OTHER RESOURCES

City of Tallahassee Official Website: Here you will find useful information about the local community and surrounding county. www.talgov.com.

Leon County Official Website: Here you will find lots of information about the community, business, and local government. www.co.leon.fl.us.

Sports Beat: This is a great place to get the latest running gear and find out about Tallahassee's upcoming races and events. Although Sports Beat is not a specialty running store, they have a large selection of running shoes and clothing. The store is located in the Westwood Shopping Center at 2020 West Pensacola Street, about a mile west of FSU's Doak Campbell Stadium (Sports Beat is located between Eckerd and the Publix supermarket). For more information call (888) 576-3334, or visit www.sportsbeatinc.com.

***Tallahassee Democrat* Online:** A great source for the latest news, happenings, and general information about the Tallahassee area. You will find lots of useful stuff including a calendar of events, services lists, and visitor links at www.tallahasseedemocrat.com.

Tallahassee Visitors' Guide: This is the official visitor's guide website for Tallahassee, Leon County, and the surrounding counties. It contains a wealth of information about upcoming events, restaurants, lodging, attractions, shopping, and nightlife. www.seetallahassee.com.

39

PANAMA CITY AREA

Emerald waters, miles of powdery, white sand beaches, and great year-round climate have made this Gulf Coast city one the most popular beach destinations in Florida. Located along the scenic US 98 highway, Panama City is a magnet for visitors from all over the world and a host to hundreds of thousands of college students that flock to this area yearly during the Spring Break celebration.

Running takes on a new dimension in this city. Not only can you run and race along pristine beaches and historic neighborhoods like St. Andrews, but you can also swim in calm waters and bike on gentle roads. In other words, you can enter one of Panama City's top-notch triathlons including the Emerald Coast Triathlon series, Gulf Coast Triathlon, Cape San Blas Duathlon, and Ironman Florida. If triathlons are

not your thing, Panama City hosts several great running-only events throughout the year. Below you will find some of the best ones.

Beautiful Beach Drive, Panama City

BEST PLACES TO RUN

Beach Drive Area: Located in Panama City, this scenic road extends from Frankford Avenue in the historic St. Andrews area to 6th Street near the center of town. Beach Drive is a shaded road with beautiful residential neighborhoods on one side and the St. Andrews Bay on the other. There is a sidewalk on the north side of the road. For a short but stimulating run, start from James R. Asbell Park located on Beach Drive and East Caroline Boulevard. There is a small public parking area next to the park on East Caroline Boulevard. From this point run east on Beach Drive until you get to 6th Street. At Beach Drive and 6th Street turn back the same way you came. This loop is about two miles long. For a longer run keep going on Beach Drive past 6th Street as it swerves right into the downtown area. Turn right on Harrison Avenue, and one block ahead is Government Street. You will find the Marina Civic Center, City Hall, and City Marina right ahead. This stretch would add an additional mile to your run. Bring water, and watch for traffic.

Panama City Beach Pier: The Dan Russell or City Pier is located on 16101 Front Beach Road, across from Aaron Bessant Park. The pier is a great spot to start your run. Here you will find free parking, restrooms, showers, and water. From this point you can literally run for miles in either direction on the world famous beach with its dazzling Gulf waters. So whether you are planning a short run or a long one, this is the place to do it. The best times to run on the beach are during early morning, evening, and low tide. If going for a long run, bring water and wear sunscreen, since the sun can be unforgiving, especially at peak hours. The nice thing about running on the beach is that you can always cool off in the water after the run. There is a small admission fee to walk on the pier, but beach access is free. The public access and facilities are located next to the pier entrance area. The parking lot is across the street. For more information about the pier call (850) 233-5080.

BEST LOCAL RACES

Mardi Gras 5K: This race is held in February in Panama City. The 5K run is the kick-off event of the Mardi Gras festivities in the St. Andrews area. There is a one-mile fun run following the 5K event.

After the races there are plenty of activities in the area such as games, sidewalk sales, food, music, and a parade. The party picks up after the parade and continues into the evening hours. Here you have a fun way to celebrate Mardi Gras and be part of the festivities in this historic neighborhood.

Race Judicata 5K: This event is held in May during Law Week in downtown Panama City. There is a 5K run and a fun run. Both races start by the Bay County Courthouse located on East 4th Street. There is an awards celebration after the events. The proceeds from the race are donated to a local charity. This is a great opportunity to run and support a good cause.

Midnight Chase 5K: This event is held on Labor Day weekend in Panama City. The 5K race starts one minute after midnight in front of the Marina Civic Center and goes through the downtown area to finish at the City Hall. The course is flat and fast. A one-mile fun run is held after the main race. Awards are given to the top three runners in each age group. This is definitely an unusual 5K and a great chance to try something new.

Tricker Trek 10K: This race is held in October during Halloween weekend. The 10K run starts by the Marina Civic Center in downtown Panama City. The course is flat and fast. There is a one-mile family fun run after the main event. This 10K can be used as a stepping stone in your fall conditioning. Plus, it's fun. There is even a costume contest. Before you go trick-or-treating, check this one out.

Draggin' Tail 18-Mile Run and Relay: This unique race is held in November in Sunny Hills, a small planned community off SR 77 in Washington County, about 35 miles north of Panama City. The race consists of teams of three, each running a six-mile stretch. The paved course is scenic and very challenging, going over rolling hills and through oak and pine forests. The race starts by the community center. If you are looking for a tough race, consider this one. You won't be alone: every year over one hundred participants enter this race. The experience will be worth the drive.

RUNNING CLUBS

Panhandle Runners & Triathlete's Club: This is a local club of runners, swimmers, bikers, and triathletes. They sponsor several events throughout the year. A membership fee is required to join. For more information write to them at PO Box 381, Panama City, FL, 32402 or visit www.knology.net/~panhandlerunner.

OTHER RESOURCES

Bay County Official Website: Offers lots of useful information about the community. www.co.bay.fl.us.

Panama City Official Website: It contains lots of information and links. www.cityofpanamacity.com.

Panama City Beach Convention and Visitors Bureau: Here you can find a visitors' guide, maps, and other useful information about Panama City Beach. Call them at (800) PCBEACH or write to: PO Box 9473, Panama City Beach FL 32417. www.800pcbeach.com.

Panama City Beaches Chamber of Commerce Website: Offers lots of community-related information, including a calendar of events, vacation planner, and business addresses. www.pcbeach.org.

***Panama City News Herald* Online:** This is the site to check for the latest local news and events. www.newsherald.com.

Steve's Bike Shop: This store offers triathlon equipment and has a good selection of running gear. They are located at 1926 W. 23rd Street in Panama City. For more information call (850) 769-6808 or visit www.biketool.com.

 **FORT WALTON BEACH AREA**

This is a charming and vibrant Gulf community located in the heart of the Emerald Coast, about thirty-two miles east of Pensacola Beach. With over 340 days of sunshine per year, the Fort Walton Beach area is an ideal place for year-round outdoor enjoyment. The local running community is very active and well organized, offering weekly group training runs as well as several interesting races throughout the year. Although this is mainly a beach-oriented town, you will find many other wonderful places to run such as historic districts, residential areas, and quite a few trails.

BEST PLACES TO RUN

Destin Beaches: Located only a few miles east of Fort Walton Beach, Destin is one of the most popular beach resorts in the Panhandle. Here you will find many ample miles of beach to run on. All you need to do is look for the signs that say "Beach Access," and running you go. Remember to hydrate and wear sunscreen. A nice place to start your run is at James Lee Park off Scenic Highway 98 in Destin. Here you will find free parking, picnic tables, restrooms, water, and plenty of beach access. From this point you can run east or west for several miles. If running on sand is not your thing, there are many quiet residential streets west of Destin's downtown area and north of US 98. Most of these streets have sidewalks, and are partly shaded. A group of local runners meets Monday evenings at McGuire's Irish Pub for a run through the surrounding area.

Henderson Beach State Park: This is a beautiful beach park located at 17000 Emerald Coast Parkway, or US 98, in Destin. It is a great place to go for a run and relax on the beach after. Both the white sand and the Gulf water will soothe your spirit and your legs, and if you wish to stay longer the park has full camping facilities. There are picnic tables, a playground, bath house, restrooms, and water. There is also a bike trail and a beach boardwalk. A small admission fee is required. The park is open every day from 8 A.M. until sundown, unless you are camping overnight. For more information, call the Henderson Beach State Park at (850) 837-7550 or visit www.dep.state.fl.us/parks/district1/hendersonbeach.

Scenic 30-A Trail: The Scenic 30-A Trail is located about twenty-eight miles east of Fort Walton Beach's center. The off-road trail starts east of Road 83 and Highway 30-A, extending from Big Redfish Lake in Blue Mountain Beach to Inlet Beach near the intersection with US 98. The eight-foot-wide path is located on the south side of the road and is shared by bikers, skaters, hikers, and joggers. Much of the thirteen-mile paved trail goes through secluded woodlands and along coastal lakes, but it also passes through several popular resorts in Grayton Beach, Seaside, Seagrove Beach, Seacrest Beach, and Rosemary Beach. The area is very beautiful and pristine with parts of the trail bordering the water of small inlets and granting spectacular views of the Gulf of Mexico at other points. There are a few bridges where the trail merges with the road, so use caution when running on these. Most of the trail is clearly marked with yellow signs. Follow them when running through the town centers, since there the path merges with the pedestrian sidewalk. The 30-A Trail is a great place to run, especially if you are staying in one of the towns along its path. There are no public facilities along the trail. Make sure to bring water. For more information about Highway 30-A including an interactive map of the trail check the "Friends of Scenic 30-A" website at www.30-a.com.

Miracle Strip Parkway: Miracle Strip Parkway is the same as US 98, which crosses Fort Walton Beach west to east. For an easy run through the town's beautiful historic and business district, start from the corner of Miracle Strip Parkway and Perry Avenue. There is parking across the street at the Publix shopping center also known as "Shoppes at Paradise Pointe" plaza. Run west on Miracle Strip Parkway. The south sidewalk, which is closer to the water, has fewer crossings. Continue running until you get to the intersection with Wright Parkway. There is an IHOP restaurant on the left side of the road. At this point turn back and retrace your steps. This loop is about four miles. Be mindful of traffic and pedestrians.

Okaloosa Island Beach: If you are looking for a nice beach run, Okaloosa Island offers a beautiful beach with lots of sand. To run on the beach start by the Okaloosa Island Pier. The pier is one of the locals' favorite spots and is located off Highway 98 about a mile east from the Brooks Bridge. Here you will find parking and plenty to see. From the pier area you can run a couple of miles in either direction. The sand is sugar-white, the water emerald, and the view hard to beat. This is definitely a great run, especially early in the morning or evening.

Okaloosa Island Loop: A great place to run is along Santa Rosa Boulevard in Okaloosa Island, but public parking can be a problem, especially if you are not staying at one of the beach resorts. One way to get around this is to start your run from the "Shoppes at Paradise Pointe" shopping plaza on Miracle Strip Parkway and Perry Avenue on the western side of the Brooks Bridge. This is the Publix and Waffle House shopping center. Here you will find parking, restrooms and food. Start your run on the south sidewalk since you will be turning right after the bridge. Be extra careful crossing Miracle Strip

The Brooks Bridge to Okaloosa Island, Fort Walton Beach

Parkway. Traffic tends to be busy. Run across the Brooks Bridge heading east. The bridge has a sidewalk—use it. Over the bridge you will get an awesome view of the Gulf Intracoastal Waterway and the Choctawhatchee Bay. As you reach the other side of the bridge, the sidewalk ends on a grassy area. Carefully veer to the right, cross the service road, and continue past the gas station. Santa Rosa Boulevard is the first right after the bridge. The sidewalk is on the north side of the road. Santa Rosa Boulevard is a two-mile stretch parallel to the Gulf behind a strip of beachfront resorts and condos. Stay on Santa Rosa Boulevard until it ends by the Eglin Air Force Base gates. At this point run back the same way you came. This loop is 4.6 miles from the eastern side of the Brooks Bridge and 5.2 miles from the Publix shopping plaza.

Shalimar Ballpark: Shalimar is a quiet neighborhood along Eglin Parkway (Road 85) just a few miles north of the center of town in Fort Walton Beach. The Shalimar Little League Ballpark located on Fourth Avenue and Eighth Street is a great place to start your run. Here you will find public parking and restrooms. From this point it is easy to run in any direction and loop around the residential streets to finish at the park. There is no sidewalk, but traffic is slow. For an easy run, head east on Fourth Avenue past Eighth Street. Keep going straight. After 12th Street, Fourth Avenue becomes Country Club Road as you enter the Country Club residential area. There will be a couple of slopes ahead. Continue on Country Club Road until you see the gated entrance to Shalimar Pointe. Turn back near the gates and head for the park the same way you came. This loop is about two miles. This area is a popular running spot among locals, especially on weekends.

Timber Lake Trail Area: This is a beautiful nature preserve located within Eglin Air Force Base boundaries just outside Fort Walton Beach. The area has a small lake, a campground, and a maze of trails totaling over twenty-six miles. Each of the trails is well marked, even for degree of difficulty. The area is great for hiking, running, and biking. The trails are well maintained but secluded. Bring water, and wear bug repellent. Watch out for wildlife, bikes and tree roots. The Timber Lake Trailhead is located on Road 234, only a few yards from Lewis E. Turner Boulevard. From Fort Walton Beach take Lewis E. Turner Boulevard (SR 189) heading east. Keep going past the Fort Walton Beach Fairgrounds and Mooney Road. Road 234 will be on your left about 1.5 miles after Mooney Road. You should see a small sign indicating the Timber Lake Pond area right next to the turn. The trailhead parking area is right there. There are several picnic tables, and a detailed map of all the trails. The Timber Lake Pond and campground area are located a little further down off Road 234. Just follow the signs to this entrance. A $5 yearly Eglin AFB permit is required to use the trails. This can be obtained at the Jackson Guard in Niceville, or by calling (850) 882-4164. The Timber Lake area is a local favorite and the yearly site of a couple of popular races. This is a wonderful place to do trail running.

BEST LOCAL RACES

Trailblazer Run: This unique trail run is held in April at the Timber Lake area in Fort Walton Beach. This 9K event is one of the area's best runs. The race starts and finishes at the Timber Lake Campgrounds. The course passes a nearby lake and continues through the wooded hillside trails. There are several obstacles (such as fallen trees), many turns, and a few water crossings. After the hard run there is a picnic for everyone at the camping area. The race is free to Northwest Florida Track Club members, and there is a small fee for non-members. The Timber Lake Campgrounds are located off Road 234 and Lewis Turner Boulevard (SR 189). If you ever wanted to run a real trail race, try this one. You won't regret it.

Billy Bowlegs 5K: This is a popular, late-evening event held in early June. The 5K is part of the traditional Billy Bowlegs festival celebration. The festival refers to eighteenth-century buccaneer William Augustus Bowles, who is said to have used the area as a pirate's playground (and not to the Seminole chief known by the same name). The race starts and finishes by the Fort Walton Beach High School located at 400 Hollywood Boulevard SW. This is a great event, and after the race there is a fun party at a nearby hotel. If you ever enjoyed pirate stories, try this one.

Mid-Bay Bridge Run: This unique event is held in late September over the Mid-Bay Bridge connecting Destin and Niceville. The race is 4.5 miles long and it starts on the south side, or Destin side, of the bridge. The run finishes on the north side of the bridge at the White Point Recreation Area in Niceville. The awards party is held at the finish area. Free transportation is provided to runners at the start and after the race. This is definitely a great run. Here you can test your endurance over this long scenic bridge while feeling inspired by the views of the Choctawhatchee Bay.

Mullet Festival 3M Run: This is an old and popular cross-country race held in October. The event takes place at the Okaloosa-Walton Community College campus in Niceville. The course is beautiful and crosses wooded trails and part of a golf course. There is a one-mile fun run before the 3M race. Become part of this local tradition by running this event next time.

McGuire's Sunset Run: This is a late afternoon race held in mid-October in Destin. There are two events, a 5K and 10K. Both races start next to McGuire's Irish Pub, which is located off US 98 across from the Tourist Information Center, and wind along the Choctawhatchee Bay. After the run head to McGuire's for the awards party. All runners get free beverages. It sounds like fun.

Timberlake Run: This event is held in November at the Timber Lake area. There are two races, a half-marathon, and a 5K. The course is paved and goes through the woods of the Eglin AFB reservation. The race starts near the intersection of Ranger Camp Road (Road 234) and Lewis Turner Boulevard (SR 189). This is a great chance to test your running condition, especially if you are preparing for the upcoming marathon season.

RUNNING CLUBS

Northwest Florida Track Club: Founded in 1973 and serving the area of Fort Walton Beach through Destin, this is a very active running club. The NWFTC offers weekly training runs and sponsors a number of trail and road races throughout the year. A membership fee is required to join. For more information write to: NWFTC, PO Box 911, Shalimar, FL, 32579, or visit www.nwftc.com.

OTHER RESOURCES

City of Destin: This website contains a wealth of information about the Destin area including news, maps, weather, and city links. www.cityofdestin.com.

City of Fort Walton Beach Official Website: Here you can find community information including a calendar of events, recreation, and government links. www.fwb.org.

Dragon Sports: This is a multi-sport store that specializes in several outdoor activities such as running, biking, and swimming. Although their running product selection is limited, this is a great place to get information about trails and local events. Dragon Sports is located at: 1130 Hospital Road in Fort Walton Beach. For inquiries call (850) 863-8612 or visit www.dragonsports.net.

Emerald Coast Convention and Visitors Bureau Website: A great site for information on lodging, restaurants, weather conditions, vacation specials, and attractions in the Fort Walton Beach and Destin area. www.destin-fwb.com.

Greater Fort Walton Beach Chamber of Commerce: Here you can find lots of information about the local area including maps, calendar of events, shopping, lodging and restaurant listings, as well as a visitors' guide. www.fortwaltonbeachfl.org.

***Northwest Florida Daily News* Online:** Covers Fort Walton Beach and several neighboring communities, and offers the latest local news and events. www.nwfdailynews.com.

PENSACOLA AREA

Pensacola, also known as the City of Five Flags, is home to the US Navy Blue Angels and the world's whitest beaches. This history-rich city is a thriving community located along the northwestern Gulf coast of Florida. Pensacola enjoys a mild sunny climate that favors outdoor activities year-round. In addition to its good weather, the area offers runners plenty of places to choose from such as beautiful beaches, historical areas, bridges, scenic paths, hilly roads, and quaint residential areas. The running community is large and very active, hosting many events throughout the year which in some cases attract thousands of runners from nearby Florida towns and southern Alabama. Whether you are a serious runner looking for new challenges or a beginner just starting out, the running options are almost endless in Pensacola.

BEST PLACES TO RUN

Blackwater Heritage State Trail: This trail is located about twenty miles northeast of Pensacola in the town of Milton. The twelve-foot-wide path is about 8.5 miles long and was built over an old railroad line. The southern trailhead is located on Stewart Street (Route 87) near the intersection with US 90 in Milton. Behind the Tastee Freeze is the trailhead entrance. Parking and restrooms are available here. From this point the trail winds north through Milton, crossing several creeks, wetlands, and Highway 191, continuing through rural areas to end at the eastern boundary of Whiting Field Naval Air Station. This is where the northern trailhead is located (Route 87-A). The trail is scenic and mostly flat. No water is available along the way, so bring your own. Watch for wildlife and be aware of road crossings. Another place you can access the trail is near the Milton Public Library, where you will also find parking and restrooms. The Blackwater Heritage Trail is a favorite local running spot and the site of a popular 5K.

Fort Pickens Area: Fort Pickens Park is located a few miles west of Pensacola Beach within the Gulf Islands National Seashore. This area is maintained by the National Park Service and requires a small admission fee. There are campgrounds, water, restrooms, nature trails, a beach, and the historic Fort Pickens. This is a favorite spot among local runners. Here you can run for several miles through the park sites and on the main road. Just be careful with traffic especially during the summer months. The park is open all year. For more information call the park visitor center (850) 934-2635 or visit the Gulf Islands National Seashore website at www.nps.gov/guis.

Fox Run Loop: Fox Run Road is a favorite local running spot. Fox Run is a beautiful residential community located about a mile west of University Parkway. Fox Run Road is on the north side of Nine Mile Road. From the corner, head north on Fox Run Road. You will pass a Mormon Church on your right and then you will enter the residential area. Keep going straight. There is no sidewalk, but traffic is slow. Fox Run Road ends at Greenbrier Boulevard. This is the one-mile mark. At this point turn back towards where you started. There are also several hilly streets off Fox Run Road that you can use to increase your mileage. Otherwise, the out and back loop is two miles.

Pensacola Beach: Located on Santa Rosa Island and only six miles south of downtown Pensacola, this is a first-class place to run. The sugary white beach extends for several miles along the transparent emerald waters. Parking is available at various points on the island, but a preferred area is by the tall ball tower on Fort Pickens Road and Pensacola Beach Boulevard across from the visitor center parking lot. Here you will find restrooms, water, and the main access to the beach. Also, the Pensacola Beach Gulf Pier is right there. This is a popular landmark with an awesome view. For a small admission fee you can walk the Pier's entire 1,471 feet into the Gulf. Using the pier as reference you can run west for 2.5 miles to the end of Pensacola Beach, or for a lot farther if you continue into the Gulf Islands National Seashore. Similarly, from the pier you can head east for at least three miles. The best times to run are during low tide or early mornings and evenings when there are fewer people around. This is not a run you want to pass up. After the workout, relax in the Gulf or check out the shops and restaurants along Pensacola Beach Boulevard.

Pensacola Junior College Track: This campus is located right next to the Pensacola Regional Airport between 9th Avenue and College Boulevard. The asphalt track is on 12th Avenue and College

Santa Rosa Trail, Pensacola Beach

Boulevard. Parking, restrooms, and water are available. This is a great place to do speed workouts or to work on your running form. For a campus map, check out the college's website, www.pjc.cc.fl.us.

Santa Rosa Trail: The Santa Rosa Trail is a paved path parallel to Fort Pickens Road in Pensacola Beach. It is a popular place to run and enjoy the ocean air and beach atmosphere. Start in front of the visitor center parking lot at the corner of Pensacola Beach Boulevard and Fort Pickens Road. Head west on Fort Pickens Road. The path is on the north side of the road. Watch for bikes and pedestrians. You will pass several condominiums and houses until the path ends at a big parking lot right near the entrance to Fort Pickens Area Gulf Islands National Seashore. At this point turn back towards the visitor center. This loop is about five miles.

Seville Quarter Area: For a historic run through Pensacola's past, visit the downtown area. Here you will find plenty to see and do after the run. The Seville Quarter is a beautiful district reminiscent of the Spanish golden era. There are many blocks of historical build-ings, restaurants, and quaint shops. This area is the site of several races every year. For a fun sightseeing run, start by Seville Square located on Government Street and Alcaniz Street. Parking may be easier on weekends and after peak hours. Head west on Government Street. Use the sidewalk, and watch for pedestrians. At about three blocks you will see Ferdinand Plaza on the left. Stay on Government Street until Spring Street. Turn right on Spring Street. Here the road will wind a little. Keep going until you get to Garden Street. Make a right on Garden Street, and continue straight until Alcaniz Street. When you get to Alcaniz Street you will see St. Michael's Cemetery across the street. At this point turn right on Alcaniz Street. Only three more blocks ahead are Government Street and Seville Square, where you started. This loop is 1.5 miles.

University of West Florida Campus: This is a beautiful campus with rolling hills and several miles of tree-lined roads. The main entrance is on University Parkway and Campus Drive Boulevard less than a mile north of Nine Mile Road. This is a great place to run and get a little hill workout. For an easy run around the inner campus perimeter, start by the Welcome Center building across from the UWF water tower. Here you will find parking, campus maps, and restrooms. Head west on Campus Drive Boulevard past the Welcome Center. Stay on the right side of the road. Use the sidewalk and watch for cars in areas where no sidewalk is available. Continue for about a mile until you get to Campus Lane. The road will get hilly, but this is good for your legs. Make a right on Campus Lane, and keep running until Campus Drive Boulevard. Make a right. You will see dormitory buildings across the street. Continue on Campus Drive Boulevard. As you near the end of the loop you will pass University Parkway on your left. The Welcome Center area is just a block ahead on your right. This loop is two miles.

University Parkway Loop: University Parkway starts at the University of West Florida's Campus Drive Boulevard and ends at Davis Highway (Road 291). University Parkway has sidewalks on both sides and goes through residential areas to more commercial ones. Starting from Campus Drive Boulevard head south towards Davis Highway. You will pass a big intersection at Nine Mile Road. There will be a large shopping center on your right. Stay on University Parkway. About one mile further you will see West Florida Hospital on your left. Continue running until University Parkway

Hilly University Parkway outside UWF, Pensacola

ends on Davis Highway. Here you will see Olive Baptist Church and a commercial center on your right. This is the 2.4–mile mark. At this point turn back the same way you came. The entire loop is 4.8 miles. For a longer run you can combine this run with the University of West Florida perimeter loop previously described.

Best Local Races

Double Bridge Run: This unique double event is held in February. It consists of two races: a 15K and a 5K. Both courses are very scenic and end in Pensacola Beach. The 15K run starts from downtown Pensacola across the Pensacola Bay Bridge through Gulf Breeze and over the Robert Sikes Bridge finishing in Pensacola Beach. The 5K run starts from the Gulf Breeze High School and goes across the Robert Sikes Bridge to end in Pensacola Beach. After the races a huge celebration party is held in Pensacola Beach. There is plenty of food, drinks, giveaway prizes, and live music. The good February weather, awesome vistas, and great party make this race hard to pass. Every year more than 2,000 runners from all ages and abilities take part of this event. If you are looking for a memorable experience, add this race to your list.

Blue Angel Marathon: This traditional event is held in February at the Naval Air Station in Pensacola. There are three races to choose from: the marathon, a half-marathon, and a 5K. All races start on Radford Boulevard inside the naval air station, but the marathon and half-marathon start an hour before the 5K. The marathon course goes through the naval base, historic downtown, and Pensacola Bay's waterfront. Although the terrain is mostly flat, you will find some rolling hills along the way. Both the half-marathon and 5K are run inside the naval air station area. The Blue Angel Marathon is a very popular event which attracts hundreds of runners every year. There is a Sports Expo that begins two days before the race. This is a great opportunity to find good deals on the latest running gear. The post-race celebration has lots of food, refreshments, and entertainment. This is definitely a nice race with something for everyone, both on the road and off.

Fiesta Run: This is an old and popular run held during the first week of May. There are two races, a 10K and 5K. Every year over a thousand runners gather at the starting line. Both races start together. The course goes from the Cordova Mall on Ninth Avenue and Bayou Boulevard to Seville Square in downtown Pensacola for the 10K. There are some challenging hills, water stations, mile splits, and music along the course. The awards party is held at Seville Square where you will find plenty of food, refreshments, camaraderie, and music. If you are looking for a traditional and fun event, this one offers all of this and more.

Bushwacker 5K: This event is held in August in Pensacola Beach. The race is part of the Bushwacker Festival, a three-day beach party with food, music, and entertainment. The 5K run starts in Gulf Breeze and finishes by the boardwalk in Pensacola Beach. This means that you get to run on the Robert Sikes Bridge and admire the view of the Santa Rosa Sound. This is a popular race attracting hundreds of runners each year, perhaps due to the fact that after the run the celebration goes on until the next day.

Marine Corps Aviation Association Run: The MCAA 5K and 10K are held in September. Both races start together on Government Street near Jefferson Street, sharing part of the course through the historic Seville Quarter in downtown Pensacola. This is a very popular event because the money raised is given to a local children's charity. Thousands of runners come out every year to support this cause and share the excitement of the road. This is a great opportunity to run for a wonderful reason.

Seafood Festival 5K: This race is held in September as part of the traditional Pensacola Seafood Festival. The 5K run wanders through the historic downtown Seville area. This is a fun race in a great setting. After the run, sample some of the best seafood around at one of the many vendors' booths. The festival has plenty of entertainment and activities for the whole family. This is one of those events where you can bring the family and not feel guilty thinking that they will be bored—here, everybody has fun.

Turkey Trot 5K: This event is held in November after Thanksgiving at the Seville Quarter. The 5K course is flat and loops through the historic downtown district. The race's proceeds go to a local scholarship fund. Following the run there is a big celebration with food, drinks, and music. This is a fun event and a terrific way to burn some of the extra calories from Thanksgiving.

RUNNING CLUBS

Pensacola Runners Association (PRA): Founded in 1972, this is one of the largest running clubs in Florida. The PRA hosts several events throughout the year including some great races. A membership fee is required to join. For more information write to: PRA, PO Box 10613, Pensacola, FL 32524, or visit www.pensacolarunners.com.

OTHER RESOURCES

City of Pensacola Official Website: It has lots of community information and links. www.ci.pensacola.fl.us.

Escambia County Official Website: Offers plenty of information about the county and several important links. www.co.escambia.fl.us.

Pensacola Beach: This is a great website maintained by the Santa Rosa Island Authority for the Pensacola Beach and Gulf Islands National Seashore area. Here you will find lodging and dining information, local news, event calendars, and maps. For questions call (800) 635-4803 or write to Santa Rosa Island Authority, PO Drawer

1208, Pensacola Beach, FL 32562. www.visitpensacolabeach.com.

Pensacola Convention and Visitor Information Center: Hosted by the Pensacola Area Chamber of Commerce, this is a good place to get useful visitor information about lodging, dining, local attractions, and event calendars. It is located off Bayfront Parkway at 1401 East Gregory Street in Pensacola. For questions call (800) 874-1234 or visit www.visitpensacola.com.

***Pensacola News Journal* Online:** Get the latest local news, entertainment, and events. www.pensacolanewsjournal.com.

Running Wild: Serving the greater Pensacola area, this store carries a complete line of running shoes and gear. This is a good place to find out more about the local running scene. Running Wild is located at 3094 Gulf Breeze Parkway in Gulf Breeze. For questions call (850) 916-7374. No website was available at the time of this publication.

CENTRAL FLORIDA

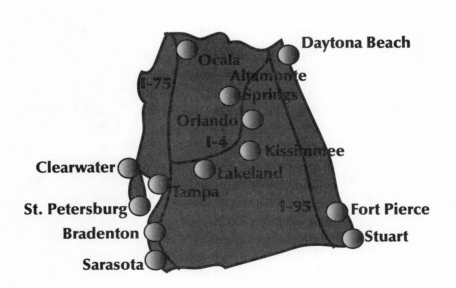

Daytona Beach

Ocala

Altamonte
Springs

I-75

Orlando

I-4

Kissimmee

Clearwater

Lakeland

Tampa

St. Petersburg

I-95

Fort Pierce

Bradenton

Stuart

Sarasota

Extending from the Atlantic Coast to the Gulf Coast, Central Florida is the state's heart and perhaps the most dynamic region with millions of people constantly moving through the area. The landscape of Central Florida is flat and sandy along the eastern coast with higher ground moving west. In fact, west of Orlando, the middle section of the region is as hilly as northwest Florida, and the many steep, rolling hills make you wonder whether you have been mysteriously transported to another state. The west coast is similar to the east and has flat and sandy terrain. Although the region is very green, the trees are not as tall as in the northern part of the state. Central Florida is known for its citrus and the hundreds of lakes that extend through the region, as well as by the many rivers originating there. As expected, the weather is a little warmer than north Florida's and a bit cooler than south Florida's. Summers are hot and humid throughout, but especially in the center where there is no sea breeze. Frequent rain showers are common in the summer and help to cool off the steamy heat. Spring, fall, and winter are all very pleasant seasons and great for outdoor activity. In the winter temperatures usually range from the high 40°s to the low 50°s. Freezing temperatures are rare.

Central Florida is not only home to some of the world's most popular family attractions, but it also has some of the state's best paved trails. Built over abandoned railroad tracks, they are well maintained and popular, offering miles of scenic natural corridors within urban areas. Additionally, the region offers state parks, off-road trails, quaint neighborhoods, historic districts, and miles of white powdery beaches on both coasts. The running scene in Central Florida is very active with many well-organized running clubs catering to what is perhaps the largest number of runners in the state. Dozens of road races and several world class events are held throughout the region every year..

Whether you live in Central Florida or are just visiting, this is a running-friendly region with endless possibilities for every preference and ability. Daytona Beach, the Space Coast, the Treasure Coast, Orlando, Lakeland, Ocala, Tampa Bay, and Sarasota are the largest running centers in Central Florida. In the following pages you will find some of the best places to run, best road races, and most useful reference information about each of the above running areas.

Daytona Beach Area

The Daytona Beach area is a great place to visit and run. Home of world-class car racing events like the Daytona 500, the area offers a number of first-class attractions together with over twenty miles of beautiful, well-maintained beaches to run on. Runners will know that they are not only running on the world's most famous beach, but also on one of the state's best. The beach between Ormond Beach and Daytona Beach Shores is very wide, almost flat, and its hard-packed sand makes running easier on the legs.

The area enjoys great weather year-round and the running community is well organized and active. There are weekly running groups that run on the beach and the local running club hosts several popular races throughout the year. Whether you are in the Daytona Beach area for business or pleasure, head to the beach for a run. It is a one-of-a-kind experience.

BEST PLACES TO RUN

Bicentennial Park: Located on A1A in Ormond By-The-Sea, this beautiful city park extends from the Halifax River (Intracoastal Waterway) to the Atlantic Ocean. The entrance to the park is on A1A about 3.5 miles north of SR 40. As you turn into the park you will see a parking lot and restrooms next to A1A. The sports facilities and nature trails are located on the western end of the park closer to the river. Follow the paved road to reach the main facilities. Bicentennial Park is a great place to start a run along A1A. For a scenic run, head south along A1A towards Ormond Beach. Make sure to run on the sidewalk located along the west side of the road. There are a few street crossings, so be wary of turning traffic. Keep running straight until you get to Neptune Avenue which is almost three miles from the park's entrance. The sidewalk ends at Neptune Avenue. At this point turn back towards the park. This loop is six miles.

Bulow Creek State Park: This is a beautiful pristine park a few miles north of Ormond Beach. The south trailhead and main access are located at 3351 Old Dixie Highway (North Beach Street). This entrance is on the east side of the road across the street from the

Halifax Plantation residential development, about 1.2 miles south from Walter Boardman Lane or five miles north of Tomoka State Park. Here you will find plenty of parking, restrooms, and picnic tables. The seven-hundred-year-old Fairchild Oak, one of the largest live oaks in Florida, is right off the parking area. The park has two trails: the half-mile Wahlin trail, and the Bulow Woods trail. The Bulow Woods trail is 6.8 miles long and runs from the Fairchild Oak area to the Bulow Plantation Ruins State Historic site at the north end of the park. The Bulow Woods trail starts a few yards north of the parking area. Follow the signs. The area is scenic and has some awesome vegetation.

For a shorter run, head on the Bulow Woods trail north until you come up to a two-lane road. This is Walter Boardman Lane. At this point turn back the same way you came. This loop is about six miles long. The area is very wooded, so wear insect repellent. Watch for tree roots and wildlife. The trail is shared with hikers and bikers. Bring water. The park is open every day from 8 A.M. until sundown. For more information call the Bulow Creek State Park at (904) 676-4050 or check the following website: www.dep.state.fl.us/parks/district3/bulowcreek.

Highbridge Park: This is a small park located on the eastern side of the Halifax River (Intracoastal Waterway) on Highbridge Road in Ormond Beach. This beautiful part of Volusia County is the site of two very popular races, the Tomoka Four-Miler and the Paul de Bruyn Memorial Run (see page 67 for additional race information). From the parking area, run east for about a hundred yards and turn left on John Anderson Drive, which is a narrow but very scenic road which runs parallel to the Halifax River and is used by many bicyclists. There are no sidewalks in this area, and extra caution should be used despite the slow traffic. Continue running south. After a mile and a half you will see houses along the road. Keep going straight. Go past Pelican Dunes until you get to Seabridge Park. This is a small park next to the river. At this point turn back and retrace your steps to Highbridge Park. This loop is four miles. The park has parking and restrooms. Bring water and consider running this rather solitary loop with a friend. Highbridge Road is about nine miles north of SR 40 on A1A or five miles south of SR 100 on A1A. The park is less than three hundred yards west of A1A right before the drawbridge.

Highbridge Road: Another scenic run from Highbridge Park is to head west on Highbridge Road through the eastern section of Bulow Creek State Park. Go over the small draw bridge and continue straight along Highbridge Road. About a mile from the park, Highbridge Road will veer right. The area is very beautiful—you will see the Bulow Creek on your right and a canopy of trees over the road. Keep going about a half-mile further until Highbridge Road ends on Walter Boardman Lane. When you get to Walter Boardman Lane turn back and run to Highbridge Park. This loop is about 3.5 miles. Highbridge Road is about nine miles north of SR 40 on A1A or five miles south of SR 100 on A1A. Highbridge Park is less than three hundred yards west from A1A right before the draw bridge. Parking and restrooms are available at the park, but no water. This route is solitary, so consider running it with a friend.

Ormond Beach Area: A great place to run is on Ormond Beach starting at Granada Boulevard. Take Granada Boulevard (SR 40) east past A1A and you will see the entrance to the beach. Here you can drive onto the beach and park in the designated area. From Granada Boulevard you can run north or south for many miles without any disruption. The beach is very wide and flat, perfect for running. A favorite run is to head south towards the Daytona Beach Main Street Pier and back. The scene is captivating with the view of the Atlantic on one side, the ample smooth beach in front, and the never-ending row of buildings and houses lining the way. This loop is about ten miles. Bring water and wear sunscreen. There are public restrooms next to the beach entrance on Granada Boulevard by the small Oceanfront Park.

Ormond Beach/Halifax River Area: A nice run is along either side of the Halifax River south of Granada Boulevard (SR 40). Free parking and public restrooms can be found at the Ormond Beach Regional Library located on Tomoka Avenue and S Beach Street, on the western side of the river. For a short run around this historic area, start from the library parking lot, head towards S Beach Street, and make a right. Use the sidewalk. Here you will have a beautiful view of the Halifax River. Stay on S Beach Street until Division Avenue and turn right. This is a quiet residential area. Make another right on

Ridgewood Avenue and continue straight. Turn right on Tomoka Avenue and the library parking lot will be just ahead. This loop is about 1.5 miles. For a longer run from the library area, you may head one block north to Granada Boulevard and turn east to cross the half-mile long Granada Bridge. Use the sidewalk on the bridge. To continue along the river, turn right after the bridge on Riverside Drive. This is a scenic road. Watch for traffic.

Spring to Spring Trail: This is a beautiful canopied oak trail on the western end of Volusia County. The 1.3-mile multi-use paved trail is closed to motorized vehicles and connects Gemini Springs Park with the DeBary Hall Historic site. If you are looking for something different, this is a nice place to get in touch with nature in an urban setting. The trail is open daily from sunrise to sunset. Admission is free. The trail is located about thirty miles southwest of Daytona Beach in the town of DeBary. Take I-4 west to the DeBary/Deltona Exit. As you leave the interstate turn west onto Dirksen Drive towards DeBary. Parking is available on Dirksen Drive just west of the entrance to Gemini Springs Park and about 200 yards before the intersection with US 17/92. The trail starts behind the parking lot.

Sunglow Pier: For a memorable run along the world's most famous beach, the Sunglow Pier is a great place to start. The pier is

located a little less than a half-mile south of Dunlawton Avenue across from Phillis Avenue in Daytona Beach Shores. There is free public parking at the Sunglow Hotel lot. Just follow the signs. The pier and beach access are right next to the hotel.

Run on the world's most famous beach, Daytona Beach

Using the pier as reference, you can run for miles in any direction. For an inspiring run along this beautiful beach, head north towards the Hilton Hotel and at that point turn back toward the pier. The Hilton is right on the beach. This loop is 5.6 miles. For a scenic long run, head north past the Hilton Hotel until you get to the Daytona Main Street Pier and turn back. This loop is about 12.6 miles. Bring water with you, especially if you are doing the long run. The beach area is a favorite spot among local runners, and is definitely a "must" run if you are visiting the area.

Trails Area/Nova Road: This is a beautiful residential area which has rolling hills and shaded streets and is located off Nova Road in Ormond Beach. The best place to start is the city Recreation Center located at the corner of Main Trail and Nova Road. The main entrance to the recreation area is right after the Trails Shopping Center on the same side of the street going north. The park has restrooms, a playground, and plenty of parking. From the parking lot run west on Main Trail towards the Trails residential area, away from Nova Road. Traffic here is usually slow, but be cautious. Use the sidewalk whenever available. Continue straight on Main Trail past the small creek, and turn right on Shady Branch/Circle Oaks. Keep going until you come to a small triangular plaza on your left side. Circle around this triangle and head back the way you came on Shady Branch/Circle Oaks. Turn left on Main Trail, and go over the little bridge. Make a left on Rio Pinar Trail, and continue on this street. There are no sidewalks in this area. At about half a mile you will enter the Tomoka Oaks Development. Continue on Rio Pinar Trail until you come to Baywood Drive. Make a left and then another left on River Bluff Drive. Keep going until Forest Oak Drive. Make a left and then a right on Rio Pinar Trail. Stay on Rio Pinar Trail heading back towards Main Trail. Make a left on Main Trail and continue straight. The park entrance will be a little over half a mile on the left side. This loop is 4.4 miles. This area is very scenic and a popular place among local runners.

BEST LOCAL RACES

Sandpiper 5K: This popular race is held in March at the Trails community in Ormond Beach. The 5K event starts by the city

Recreation Center off Main Trail and Nova Road and finishes at the Trails Shopping Center across the street. The course meanders through the rolling and beautiful tree-lined streets of the Trails residential community. There is also a one-mile fun run held along with the 5K race. An awards party with food and drinks takes place after the run. This is a great event on a beautiful course. The Trails Shopping Center and Trails Community are located on Nova Road about ¼ mile north of SR 40.

Easter Beach Run: This classic race is held in late March or early April in Daytona Beach. The date usually falls on the day before Easter, sometimes a week earlier. There are two events: a two-mile run for kids under age twelve, and a four-miler open to all ages. Both races start and finish on the beach under the Main Street Pier. The course is on hard-packed sand and goes north and back. Following the runs there is a post-race celebration, where age group awards go ten deep and there is plenty of food and refreshments for everyone. The Easter Beach Run is not only a popular event but also one of Florida's oldest races. If you are looking for a great family event, consider this one.

Race for the Cure 5K: This race is held in May at the Daytona International Speedway in Daytona Beach. There are three coed events, all held inside the speedway: the main 5K run, a 2.5-mile non-competitive race, and a one-mile fun run. Following the races there is an awards ceremony with food, drinks, and prize drawings. This has become a very popular event which attracts over two thousand runners each year. Proceeds from the race benefit breast cancer research. Here you have a unique opportunity to support a good cause and run at one of the world's most famous speedways. The Daytona International Speedway is located on International Speedway Boulevard about two miles east of I-95.

Firecracker Ten-Miler: This event is held in June in Daytona Beach. There are two runs: the ten-mile main race, and a 5K. Both events start and finish on the beach by the Main Street Pier. The ten-mile course goes north for five miles into Ormond Beach and then turns back to the pier. After the races a fun awards celebration is held, and there is food and drinks for everyone. Although a ten-mile race on the beach can be a challenging run, it is also a great chance to test your endurance, and what better place to do it than on the world's most famous beach.

Tomoka Four-Miler: This traditional event is held during the second half of September in Ormond Beach. The four-mile run starts and finishes at Highbridge Park located next to the Intracoastal Waterway on Highbridge Road. The course is flat and very scenic along Highbridge Road. This is a winding asphalt road lined with palm trees, magnolias, and live oaks which borders marshes and the Tomoka River tributaries. Following the race, the awards celebration is held at the park, with plenty of food and drinks for everyone. The Tomoka Four-Miler is not only a beautiful run, it is also among the oldest continuous races in the State. Every year runners from North and Central Florida meet at the starting line to run this popular event. If you are looking for a great race in a natural setting, try this one. Bring insect repellent since sometimes mosquitoes can be a problem in this area.

Paint the Towne 5K: This event is held in October in Daytona Beach. There is a 5K race and a one-mile fun run. The 5K starts and finishes by The Art League of Daytona Beach building and loops through the historic streets of Old Daytona. Following the run there is a fun awards party which offers food, drinks, and entertainment for everyone. This race is held in conjunction with the Art Happening Festival, so you can stick around for more colorful activities such as art exhibits, face painting, and quick portraits. If you are looking for a beautiful run and a family event consider this one. The Art League of Daytona Beach is located at 433 South Palmetto Avenue, one block east of US 1, in Daytona Beach.

Paul de Bruyn Memorial Run: This unique event is held in November in Ormond Beach. It consists of two races: a 15K, and the main 30K event. Both races start together at Highbridge Park. The course is flat and meanders through scenic, tree-canopied roads along marshes and river tributaries to finish back at Highbridge Park. The Paul de Bruyn run is a very popular event in this part of Florida, a running tradition since the early 1970s. Following the races there is a huge awards celebration with food, drinks, and entertainment for everyone—and even free pasta for all runners. This is definitely a one-of-a-kind event in beautiful surroundings. Highbridge Park is on

Highbridge Road right next to the Intracoastal Waterway. Highbridge Road is located off A1A about nine miles north of SR 40.

RUNNING CLUBS

Daytona Beach Track Club: Started in 1973, this is one of the oldest running clubs in Florida. The DBTC is a very active and organized group which hosts several races throughout the year. A membership fee is required to join the club. For more information write to: DBTC, PO Box 1303, Daytona Beach, FL 32115, or visit www.daytonatrackclub.org.

OTHER RESOURCES

City of Ormond Beach Official Website: It contains useful information about the community. www.ormondbeach.org.

Daytona Beach Area Convention & Visitors Bureau: The official visitor information site for the Daytona Beach area, which offers information about the local weather, where to stay, where to eat, what to do, and a myriad of other things. www.daytonabeach.com.

***Daytona Beach News-Journal* Online:** Get the local news, weather, entertainment, and events. www.n-jcenter.com.

The Chamber of Daytona Beach: This site contains lots of useful information about the Daytona Beach and Halifax area such as a calendar of events, list of businesses, community news, and visitor information. www.daytonachamber.com.

Volusia County Government: Here you can find lots of great information about Volusia County's beaches, parks, tourism, and weather. www.volusia.org.

SPACE COAST AREA

Home to Cape Canaveral and to NASA's space shuttle program, this beautiful area encompasses the thriving communities of Titusville, Cocoa, Cocoa Beach, and Melbourne. The Space Coast area is a first-class destination for running and leisure which offers plenty of things to see and do, such as watching the space shuttle launch and relaxing at the beach. Runners will find a number of great places to run here, among them the corridor along the Indian River (Intracoastal Waterway), several historic neighborhoods, parks, and the pristine beaches of the Atlantic shore. The local running club does a great job of keeping the large running community active by organizing several races throughout the year, among them Florida's oldest—the Space Coast Marathon.

BEST PLACES TO RUN

Cocoa Beach Area: A convenient place to begin a run in Cocoa Beach is from Second Street and Atlantic Avenue (A1A). When the tide is low you can run on the beach for several miles in either direction. When the tide is high you can do a sightseeing run through the surrounding neighborhood including Cocoa Isles, a beautiful residential area only a few blocks west of the beach. Also, the Up & Running store is located on Atlantic Avenue half a block north from the beach access at Second Street. Here you can get more information about running in the beach area.

Indian River Drive: This is a scenic residential road which borders the western edge of the Indian River and extends over seven miles between US 1 and King Street (SR 520). The best place to find parking is at the Central Brevard Public Library located at 308 Forrest Avenue. The parking lot entrance is by the side of the library on Mulberry Street. Here you will find restrooms and parking. From the parking lot run east on Mulberry Street towards Indian River Drive (half a block away) and turn left. You will be going north on Indian River Drive. Use the sidewalk when available. The scenery is right out of a magazine: beautiful homes, oak trees, colorful gardens, small rolling hills, and the river on one side. Keep going straight past Dixon Boulevard. Mc Farland Park is right across the road from Coquina Drive. This is a small public park next to the river and another place to find parking (but without restrooms). If at this point you turn back towards the library, this loop will be 5.2 miles.

For a longer run continue north on Indian River Drive. The sidewalk ends two blocks after the park at Mc Farland Drive. Traffic here is slow, but be cautious anyway. Keep going past River Heights Road.

A little further you will go under the ramp of SR 528. Here the road winds a little. Stay on Indian River Drive. Turn left on River Point Drive and make another left on Westchester Drive. This is a one-mile hilly loop. Stay on Westchester Drive past Nottingham Lane and past High Point Drive. The road will veer right. Make a right on High Point Drive and a left on Westchester Drive. You will be going downhill. Make a right on River Point Drive and after one more block you will be back on Indian River Drive. If at this point you decide to turn back, this loop will be 8.2 miles.

Otherwise, turn left on Indian River Drive and continue north. Go past Twin Lakes Road and past Briarwood Lane. The road narrows a little but traffic is not bad. Continue running straight, and go past Blacks Road. At this point you will be about a mile from where Indian River Drive ends. Keep going until you come to the intersection with US 1 and an old firehouse building on the right side. This is the north end of Indian River Drive. At this point turn back and head straight towards the library. This long loop is about 13.8 miles. Whether you want to do a short run or a long one, this is definitely a great place to do it. Remember to bring water, especially if you are going for the long run.

South Tropical Trail Area: This is a popular and idyllic residential area located in Indian Harbour Beach along a thin stretch of land between the Banana River and the Indian River. For an inspiring run start from the corner of Banana River Drive and SR 513, and head west along Banana River Drive. After a few blocks you will see the Mathers Bridge. Continue across the small draw bridge, and veer right as you come to the other side. This is the start of the scenic South Tropical Trail. Here the road is very narrow and speed bumps keep traffic slow. There are no sidewalks, so you will have to share the road with the few cars and bicycles. Watch your step over the bumps. For the most part you will be running alongside the Indian River, and in some sections you will be almost next to the water. The view is spectacular. Continue north on South Tropical Trail until you see the underpass of the Pineda Causeway (SR 404). Turn back on the grassy area before the underpass and head south retracing your path to where you started. This loop is ten miles. Many locals park their vehicles at The Pines condos parking lot located next to the gas sta-

Popular South Tropical Trail, Indian Harbour Beach

tion on the northwest corner of Banana River Drive and SR 513. This is a couple of blocks east of the Mathers Bridge. If you go there, try to park closest to the gas station and away from the condos. Bring water and watch for traffic. Enjoy the run.

Wickham Park: This is a popular city park located in Melbourne. The park's entrance is on Parkway Drive about a half-mile east of Wickham Road. The park has several grassy fields, playgrounds, a small lake, a horse track with stables, a nature trail, picnic areas, a campground, restrooms, free parking, and a paved perimeter road 1.3-miles long. This park is the site of several local races and a favorite running spot among locals. The park's convenient location makes it a good place to find parking and run in the surrounding neighborhood. For a great run outside the park, start from the parking lot located right off the entrance in front of the ranger's office. Head out of the park, and turn right on Parkway Drive. Use the sidewalk. Turn right on Wickham Road, and continue straight. You will go by the Brevard Community College campus. Make a right on Post Road right after the BCC buildings. Stay on Post Road.

71

Wickham Park, Melbourne

Go past Sherwood Elementary School, and turn right on Croton Road. Here the sidewalk is located on the east side of the road. Continue for about a mile and make a right on Parkway Drive. The entrance to Wickham Park is half a mile away. This loop is 4.2 miles from the parking lot near the entrance. An easy way to increase the mileage of the run is to continue around the perimeter of the park. If you do this, the total mileage will be about 5.5 miles. The park is open daily from 7 A.M. to sunset.

BEST LOCAL RACES

Eye of the Dragon 10K: This unique event is held in January in Melbourne. There are two races: the 10K run and a two-mile fun run. Both races start and finish at Pineapple Park on Highland Avenue. The main course goes east over the Eau Gallie Causeway (SR 518) and back. After the race there is an awards party with food, drinks, and fun for everyone. If you are looking for a challenging and scenic event, this race offers both. The view of the Indian River is spectacular and you will definitely get a good workout climbing the bridge. This race has consistently been voted the Space Coast's event of the year.

Tiger Dash Run: This popular event is held in February in Melbourne. There are two main races: a 5K and a 10K. Also there is a one-mile fun run and a ? mile run for little kids. The races start and finish between the Wickham Park Pavilion and the Brevard Community College parking lot off Wickham Road. The course is flat and loops through the surrounding streets; the 10K goes through Wickham Park as well. After the events there is a fun awards party with food, refreshments, and door prizes. With its many options, this event is perfect for the whole family, whether they come as spectators or decide to enter one of the runs.

Space Walk of Fame 8K: This race is held in March in Titusville. In the past this traditional event was held in April as part of the Indian River Festival. The race starts about a block from Space View Park on Indian River Avenue and Broad Street and finishes at the park. The course is flat, mostly shaded, and follows the Indian River. After the race there is an awards celebration at Space View Park which offers food, drinks, and door prizes. For many years this has been one of the most popular events in the area, so if you are looking for proven success try this one.

Melbourne Art Festival 5K: This run is held in April as part of the Melbourne Art Festival celebration. The 5K race starts and finishes at Holmes Park in the historic downtown area. From the park, runners head east along Crane Creek, cross the Melbourne Causeway over the beautiful Indian River, and turn back. This event has become one of the most popular on the Space Coast attracting several hundred runners every year. Because the race is held during the Art Festival there is usually a crowd of spectators cheering runners along the course. Following the run there is a great awards party at the park with food, refreshments, and entertainment. If you decide to enter this race, sign up early to guarantee a tee-shirt, and remember to check out the art show after the awards ceremony.

Pumpkins in the Park 5K: This picturesque event is held in late October in downtown Cocoa. The 5K race starts at Riverfront Park in Cocoa Village and loops through the quaint historic area. After the race there is a fun awards celebration with food and refreshments for everyone. This is a popular event in a beautiful place.

Space Coast Classic 15K: This run is held in early November in Melbourne Beach. The 15K race starts at Ryckman Park on Ocean Avenue and meanders through beautiful Melbourne Beach residential streets of. The course is flat and fast. Following the run, the awards party has plenty of food and drinks for all. If you are looking for more miles than a 5K but less than a marathon, this may be the best choice. Plus, this race has been voted event of the year by the local club.

Space Coast Marathon: Held in November in Cocoa, this is Florida's oldest marathon. The event consists of two races: the marathon and a half-marathon. The scenic course along Indian River Drive includes some rolling hills and a spectacular view of the Indian River. Water and aid stations are located at mile splits. The post-race party is a treat with lots of drinks, food, and entertainment for everyone. This is definitely a great event and one of Florida's ongoing running traditions. If you are looking for a low-key marathon with a challenging course, consider this one.

RUNNING CLUBS

Space Coast Runners: This large and well-established running club is based in Melbourne. The SCR offers weekly training groups and hosts several races throughout the Space Coast area every year. A membership fee is required to join. For more information write to: SCR, PO Box 2407, Melbourne, FL 32902, or visit www.spacecoas-trunners.org.

OTHER RESOURCES

Brevard County Official Website: Here you will find useful information about the area. www.countygovt.brevard.fl.us.

Cocoa Beach Area Chamber of Commerce: Here you can get information about the Cocoa Beach area, a visitors' guide, and some useful links. www.cocoabeachchamber.com.

Cocoa Beach Official Website: Here you will find a tremendous amount of information about the community, leisure activities, parks, area lodging, area dining, and city government. www.cityof-cocoabeach.com.

Florida Today **Online:** Here you will find the latest local news, weather, entertainment, sports, and events. There is also a great online visitor guide maintained by the newspaper. www.floridatoday.com.

Melbourne Area Chamber of Commerce: This website has lots of information about the Melbourne area including community profile, calendar of events, and visitor's guide.www.melpb-chamber.org.

Titusville: The Titusville Area Visitors Council hosts a great site which offers maps, a calendar of events, dining, lodging, local attractions, and much more information. www.spacecityflusa.com.

Up & Running: Based in Cocoa Beach, this is Brevard County's only running store. The store specializes in running and walking gear. Up & Running sponsors a regular weekly training program and helps organize several local races in the area. The store is located at 220 North Atlantic Avenue in Cocoa Beach (half a block north of Second Street on A1A North). For more information call (321) 799-0070 or visit www.uprunninginc.com.

TREASURE COAST AREA

The Treasure Coast stretches over a long geographic area of beautiful communities and resorts linking the central and southeastern coasts of Florida. Vero Beach, Fort Pierce, Port St. Lucie, Stuart, and Hobe Sound are just a few of the towns in this lively region.

The area is big on recreation and outdoor activities. Here you will find plenty of places to run such as parks, residential neighborhoods, historic districts, bridges, scenic A1A, and the banks of the beautiful Indian and St. Lucie Rivers. Although there are tens of miles of inviting powdery white beaches, running on these is not easy due to the high surf and steep incline that leaves little hard sand to run on. The region enjoys an excellent climate year round and is mostly flat except for the several high bridges. Many of the areas are unspoiled and the crowds are still small, making it the perfect destination for leisure and running.

The running community is spread out, but very active. The local running club hosts many popular races throughout the region.

BEST PLACES TO RUN

Babe Ruth Field: This is a small park located in a residential area of Vero Beach at the corner of 20th Avenue and 16th Street. It is a convenient place to find parking and run through the historic center of town. For an easy run, head north from the parking lot along 20th Avenue. Use the sidewalk. Keep going until 20th Street (SR 60) and turn right. Continue straight for a few blocks until 14th Avenue. Make a right on 14th Avenue. Here you will go by several antique shops. Continue past the stores and turn right on 16th Street. Stay on 16th Street past the Citrus Bowl until you get to 20th Avenue where you started. This loop is 1.8 miles.

Fort Pierce's Hutchinson Island: This island between the Indian River (Intracoastal Waterway) and Atlantic Ocean is a beautiful area to run in. Here you have a number of places to choose from along scenic paved sidewalks. Because the ocean surf in this area tends to be high, the beach itself is usually not the best choice. A good starting place is South Beach Boardwalk located on A1A about three miles southeast from the South Bridge. Here you will find free parking, restrooms, water, and access to the beach. The sidewalk is on the beach side of the road. For a short but relaxed run head south along A1A. Go past Surfside Park on your left. Continue running south until you get to the entrance of Ocean Village resort (2400 South Ocean Drive). The sidewalk ends here. At this point turn and go back to South Beach Boardwalk. This loop is about 2.6 miles. Along this section of A1A there are several quiet residential streets on the western side of the road. This is an easy way to increase your mileage and get a better view of the area.

For a longer run starting from South Beach Boardwalk head north along A1A (Ocean Drive). Stay on A1A until it turns left onto Seaway Drive. Here the paved sidewalk is on the south side (left hand) so be careful crossing the road. Continue straight on Seaway Drive towards the South Bridge. After the houses and shops there is a very scenic stretch with beautiful palm trees and green lawns lining the sidewalk. It almost makes you feel you are in a faraway trop-

Fort Pierce's Hutchinson Island

ical island. Go across the South Bridge to the other end. The view of the river and waterfront area is spectacular. When you reach the end of the bridge you will see Indian River Drive and a small park to the left of the bridge ramp. Turn at this point and head back over the bridge toward South Beach Boardwalk the same way you came. This loop is about 6.4 miles.

Fort Pierce's Jetty Park: Located at the eastern end of Seaway Drive on Hutchison Island, this beautiful waterfront park is a convenient place to park and run. From Jetty Park run west along Seaway Drive. Use the south side sidewalk. Continue past the shops and houses towards the South Bridge. Run across the South Bridge to the other end at Indian River Drive. At this point turn back over the bridge and head towards Jetty Park the same way. This loop is five miles. Another easy run from Jetty Park is to head west on Seaway Drive for about a block and turn left on Ocean Drive. Stay on Ocean Drive (A1A) past South Beach Boardwalk. Keep going straight until you get to the entrance of the Ocean Village resort. At this point turn back and retrace your way to Jetty Park. This loop is about 4.2 miles.

Jack Island State Preserve Trails: This is a beautiful mangrove island between the Indian River (Intracoastal Waterway) and North Hutchinson Island in Fort Pierce. Jack Island is located about 1.5 miles north of the Fort Pierce Inlet State Recreation Area. The access to Jack Island is on the west side of A1A. Free parking is available along the entrance road. The only way to get onto the island is over a concrete foot bridge located at the west end of the access road. When I visited, a portable restroom was available near the bridge. Jack Island has a couple of trails, the longest totaling about 4.3 miles. You will find a map of the trails by the entrance to the island. The terrain is soft and mainly a mixture of dirt, sand, and grass. The scenery is natural and very pretty with lots of trees, bushes, and some wildlife. This is a great place to do some trail running, especially since there aren't many trails available in this part of Florida. Bring water along as there is none available in the island. Sometimes bugs can be a problem, so it is best to wear insect repellent while on the trails. Jack Island is open from 8 A.M. until sundown. For more information call (772) 468-3985 or visit www.dep.state.fl.us/parks/district5/fortpierceinlet.

Jack Island State Preserve trails, Fort Pierce

Jonathan Dickinson State Park: This scenic park is a popular place among local runners. The combination of nature trails and paved roads adds up to more than six miles of terrain suitable for running. The park has two campgrounds, picnic tables, a playground, restroom facilities, a ranger station, and plenty of parking. Hikers, bikers, and horses share some of the trails, so be careful. Trail maps can be obtained at the ranger station. Jonathan Dickinson State Park is located off highway US 1 along the western side of the Intracoastal Waterway and only a few miles south of the center of town in Hobe Sound. There is a small admission fee required to get into the park. For more information call (772) 546-2771 or visit www.dep.state.fl.us/parks/district5/jonathandickinson.

Lake Okeechobee Scenic Trail (LOST): The 110-mile trail around Florida's largest lake is built mostly on dikes and is part of the Florida National Scenic Trail. The trail is open year round and shared by hikers, bikers, and joggers. The trail area is wide and easy on the feet. There are no trees along most of the trail, so you won't find shade. The best time to run is during the cooler months or early morning. Either way, wear sunscreen and bring water to be safe. Because the trail is so long you can only run small portions at a time or in between access points. There are several well-marked entry points along the roads and towns encircling the lake. Most of these are two to ten miles apart. Some of the access areas have water and facilities. Two entry points along the northeastern side of the lake are Port Mayaca Recreation Area, located at the intersection of roads SR 76 and US 441 and Okee-Tantie Recreation Area, located a few miles south of the town of Okeechobee on US 441. Both areas have parking and are located within an hour's drive from the east coast. From these points you can run as much as you want in either direction. If you are looking for a different and great experience, LOST is an unforgettable place. The view across the massive lake is awesome. For a map of the trail check the U.S. Army Corps of Engineers website at: www.saj.usace.army.mil/recreation/images/maps/lostmap.pdf.

Lawnwood Recreation Area: Located along the north side of Virginia Avenue (SR 70) in Fort Pierce, this park has several fields, dirt trails, grassy areas, restrooms, and plenty of parking. This is a convenient place to park and run through the surrounding neighborhood. For an easy run, start from the parking area and head east (left) towards Sunrise Boulevard. Use the sidewalk when available. Turn left on Sunrise Boulevard. You will go through a residential area. Stay on Sunrise Boulevard and watch for intersections. Go past Parkway Avenue. You will see a small plaza at the corner of Sunrise Boulevard and US 1. Turn right on US 1 (4th Street) and continue straight for about a mile. Turn right on Virginia Avenue. Go past Sunrise Boulevard until you see the Lawnwood Recreation Area parking lot where you started. This loop is 3.3 miles.

Riverside Park: This scenic city park located along the eastern side of the Intracoastal Waterway is a convenient place to start a run in Vero Beach. The entrance to the park is on Mockingbird Drive about two blocks south of Beachland Boulevard (SR 60). The park has a one-mile fitness trail, a playground, tennis courts, grassy areas, restrooms, water fountains, and plenty of parking. From the park you can head out into the surrounding neighborhood for a run along the shaded residential streets. Starting from the parking lot near the tennis courts, head out towards Mockingbird Drive and turn right (south). Use the sidewalk. Continue straight until Iris Lane. Make a left on Iris Lane and a right on A1A. Continue on A1A for about a mile until you reach the corner of A1A and SR 656 (East Causeway Boulevard). At this point turn back along A1A the same way you came. Stay on A1A past Iris Lane until you get to Beachland Boulevard (SR 60) and turn left. Continue straight on Beachland Boulevard past the quaint shopping area until you get to Mockingbird Drive. Make a left on Mockingbird Drive and Riverside Park will be two blocks ahead on your right. Turn into the park back to the tennis court area where you started. This loop is 3.8 miles.

For a longer run you may combine this loop with a run over the Merrill Bridge (Beachland Boulevard) across the Indian River (Intracoastal Waterway) and back. The distance from the corner of Mockingbird Drive and Beachland Boulevard to the other side of the bridge and back is 2.4 miles extra, so this combined run would be about 6.2 miles. Regardless of which loop you choose, this is definitely a great area to run.

Roosevelt Bridge Area: A popular place to run in beautiful downtown Stuart is over the old and new Roosevelt bridges. Starting from the Lyric Theater area on SW Flagler Avenue head north toward the old drawbridge. Use the sidewalk on the left side. Once across the old bridge continue straight. After about half a mile you will see the access ramp to the new bridge in front of you to your left. Access the bridge from here so that you will stay on the southbound sidewalk coming back. The new bridge is very steep but the view of the St. Lucie River is awesome. Coming down take the first right and go along the wall of the new bridge through the parking lot back to Flagler Avenue (under the new bridge). From this point you can run straight to where you started. This scenic loop is about three miles. There is free parking along Flagler Avenue in front of the Lyric Theater and under the new bridge.

BEST LOCAL RACES

Bridge Buster 5K: This traditional event is held in January in Fort Pierce. The 5K race starts from the Fort Pierce Community Center located on Indian River Drive and goes east and back over the South Causeway Bridge. The course is beautiful. Following the run there is an awards party with food and drinks for everyone. This is a popular race in the Treasure Coast area.

Sunrise 5K: This popular event is held in mid-January in Fort Pierce. The 5K race starts at the Sunrise Theatre located on 2nd Street and moves through the historic downtown across the South Causeway Bridge and back. The waterfront view of the Indian River is beautiful. A free fun run for kids is held after the 5K race. Following the events there is an awards celebration with lots of food, refreshments, and fun for all. Proceeds from this race go to benefit the historic Sunrise Theatre.

Del Hagin Memorial 15K: This run is held in early February in Hobe Sound. The 15K race starts at the Hobe Sound Elementary School located off A1A on SE Gomez Avenue and loops through the surrounding area. After the run there is a fun awards party with food and drinks. This is one of the few races longer than 10K on the Treasure Coast, so if you are looking for something more challenging consider this one.

Sunrunners 10K: This popular event is held in February in Vero Beach. The 10K starts at South Beach and runs on the street along Ocean Drive. The course is flat and fast. The view is beautiful. After the run there is an awards celebration with lots of food and refreshments. Years of tradition have made this one of the classic events in the area.

LOST 7-Miler: This unique race is held in early April in Port Mayaca. The seven-mile run starts at the Port Mayaca Recreation Area in Lake Okeechobee. The race is on the scenic trail along the eastern side of this massive lake. The view is great. After the run there is an awards party with food and drinks for everyone. This is a beautiful place and a fun race. Port Mayaca is located at the intersection of roads SR 76 and US 441, about 32 miles west of Stuart.

Run for the Pineapple 5K: This event is held in late May in Sewall's Point. This small town is located east of Stuart between the St. Lucie River and the Indian River (Intracoastal Waterway). The 5K race starts at the Sewall's Point City Hall and loops through the residential neighborhood. The course is fast and scenic. After the run, there is food and refreshments for everyone at the awards party. This is one of the most popular races in the area.

Jalapeno 5K: This popular evening 5K run is held in July in Fort Pierce at the St. Lucie County Civic Center located on Virginia Avenue. This run is part of the annual Exchange Club Chili Cook-Off weekend celebration. Following the run there is an awards celebration with food and refreshments, and all participants are invited to the chili cook-off party after the race. It is all for a worthy purpose. The proceeds from this event support a local child abuse prevention center. This race has everything: great food, free entertainment, and a good cause.

Sandsprit 5K: This event is held in September in Stuart. The 5K race starts and finishes at Sandsprit Park. The beautiful course loops south along St. Lucie Boulevard toward A1A and into the surrounding streets. Following the run there is an awards event with food and drinks for everyone. This is one of the more popular races in the area. Sandsprit Park is located next to the river off St. Lucie Boulevard and a little south of the Martin County Airport.

Jungle Jog 5K: This popular event is held in mid-October in Vero Beach. The 5K race starts and finishes at the Jungle Club Sports Complex located on 6th Avenue. After the run there is a nice awards ceremony at the club with great food, refreshments, and prizes. This is definitely a well-organized race, and the event's proceeds benefit a local charity.

Halloween 10K: This traditional run is held in late October at Jonathan Dickinson State Park in Hobe Sound. This 10K race is a popular event in the Treasure Coast area. A 5K walk is held in addition to the main run. After the events there is an awards party with food and drinks. Jonathan Dickinson State Park is located off highway US 1 a few miles south of the center of town in Hobe Sound, or about twelve miles south of Stuart on US 1. In addition to the race entry fee, a small admission charge is required to get into the park.

Dolphin Dash 5K: This event is held in early November in Vero Beach. The 5K run starts and finishes at Riverside Park located off Mockingbird Drive near Beachland Boulevard (SR 60). The course is fast, flat and beautiful. A one-mile walk event follows the 5K. After the races an awards celebration with food and refreshments is held at the park. This is a fun race.

Harbor Branch 5K: This run is held in November at the Harbor Branch Oceanographic Institution in Fort Pierce. The main entrance to the HBOI is located at 5600 US 1 North, or about six miles north of the South Causeway Bridge in Fort Pierce. The 5K certified course loops around the HBOI main campus. After the race there is an awards celebration with food and drinks. If you are looking for a popular race in a unique place this one has it all.

Jack Island Run: This unique cross-country race takes place in December in Fort Pierce. The 4.125-mile run is held at the Jack Island Preserve located between A1A and the Indian River. The entrance to Jack Island Preserve is on A1A about 1.5 miles north of the Fort Pierce Inlet State Recreation Area. The race starts and finishes on the island by the concrete foot bridge. The course is on dirt, grass, and sand trails around the island. The area is very pristine with mangrove trees, bushes, and wildlife. An awards party is held after the run with food and refreshments for everyone. If you are looking for a small event in a natural setting consider this race.

RUNNING CLUBS

Sailfish Striders: This is an active running club based in Stuart. They include a wide geographic area along the Treasure Coast from Vero Beach to Tequesta. The Sailfish Striders are known for hosting several quality races throughout the area. A small membership fee is required to join the club. For more information write to: Sailfish Striders, PO Box 1334, Stuart, FL 34995, or visit www.sailfishstriders.com.

Sunrunners of Vero Beach: This is a small but active running club based in Vero Beach. They host weekly group runs and a few races throughout the year. Runners of all abilities are welcomed. For more information write to: Sunrunners of Vero Beach, PO Box 3032, Vero Beach, FL 32964. No website was available at the time of publication.

OTHER RESOURCES

City of Vero Beach Official Website: Here you will find information about the area including places to see, calendar of events, and weather. www.vero-beach.fl.us.

***Fort Pierce Tribune* Online:** Get the latest local news, weather, entertainment, sports, and calendar of events. www.fptribune.com.

Martin County Official Website: Here you will find useful information about the area. www.martin.fl.us.

St. Lucie County Chamber of Commerce: This is a very informative website. It contains lots of community information such as points of interest, calendar of events, and a visitor's guide. www.stluciechamber.org.

St. Lucie County Official Website: Here you will find lots of information about the area as well as a great visitor's guide. www.co.st-lucie.fl.us.

***Stuart News* Online:** Here you will find local news, weather, entertainment, sports, and calendar of events. www.stuartnews.com.

***Vero Press Journal* Online:** Here you can get local news, weather, entertainment, sports, and calendar of events. www.pressjournal.com.

ORLANDO AREA

Orlando, the world's most popular vacation destination, is also a great place to run. Altamonte Springs, Apopka, Maitland, and Winter Park are just a few of the runner-friendly communities in this beautiful and bustling area. Here you will find many places to run such as parks, residential neighborhoods, historic districts, and some of Florida's best-maintained paved trails.

Although most of the popular running spots are located away from the busy tourist area, many resorts have their own nature trails and boardwalks where you can easily log a few miles and enjoy some of the best scenery around. If you are staying in one of these resorts ask the hotel staff for places to run nearby. Even when no trails are available you can usually find a private road around the resort where you can run safely.

Orlando's running community is large, active, and well-organized. There are many races held during the year as well as regular weekly training groups throughout the area. Whether you are a visitor or a resident, it is always fun to run in Orlando.

BEST PLACES TO RUN

Cady Way Trail: This urban trail runs from near the Orlando Fashion Square Mall to Showalter Field in Winter Park. The 3.5-mile trail is paved, shaded, and very pleasant, with mile markers and water fountains along the way. The best place to access the trail is its north end at Cady Way Park. This is part of Showalter Field and Ward Memorial Park. Here you will find parking, restrooms, water, picnic areas, and several sport facilities. The distance from this point to the south end of the trail and back is seven miles. For a shorter run use the mile markers to tailor your run accordingly.

Another great place to access the trail is from its south end, located on Herndon Avenue just east of the Orlando Square Fashion Mall and next to the Herndon Station Post Office, about 0.2 mile north of East Colonial Drive (SR 50). Herndon Avenue is 2.2 miles east of I-4 on Colonial Drive. This trailhead has free parking but no water or restrooms. From here you can run north as far as you want. This is a popular trail shared with bikers, skaters, and walkers, so be cautious. The trail is open daily from sunrise to sunset.

Cross Seminole Trail, Seminole County

Cross Seminole Trail: This popular multi-purpose trail is located northeast of Orlando in Seminole County. The 3.8-mile paved trail runs from Gardena Avenue in Winter Springs to downtown Oviedo. Although there are several access points, a great place to find parking and get on the trail is at the Black Hammock Trailhead. The entrance to the Black Hammock Trailhead is through a small side road off SR 434 West (south side) less than two hundred yards before the intersection with SR 417. Here you will find plenty of free parking, restrooms, water, a trail map, and a gazebo. The trail path is behind the parking lot, past the restrooms. Follow the signs. The asphalt trail is smooth, wide, and surrounded by vegetation. From Black Hammock the trail splits in two opposite directions. You can run west to the end of the trail at Gardena Avenue and back for a 3.6-mile loop, or head east to downtown Oviedo and back for a four-mile run. For a longer run, do both legs of the trail for a combined total of 7.6 miles. Many bikers, skaters, and hikers use the trail, so be cautious. The trail is open daily during daylight hours.

Little Econ Greenway Trail: This beautiful multi-purpose trail runs parallel to the Little Econ River. The trail is paved and very scenic. The spectacular view of the river will likely inspire you to run the entire length of the trail. The best place to access the LEG trail is Jay Blanchard Park located at 2451 North Dean Road, about 0.7 miles north of Colonial Drive (SR 50), in East Orlando. The entrance to the park is on the eastern side of Dean Road. Here you will find plenty of free parking, water, restrooms, a playground, picnic tables, a park office, and maps. The distance from the park office located near the eastern end of the park to the western end of the trail is four miles (near SR 50). So if you run the entire trail and back it is about an 8-mile loop. There are mile markers along the way to help you know your location. This is a very popular trail especially during afternoons and weekends. Runners will have to share the trail with bikers, skaters, and walkers. The trail is open daily from sunrise to sunset.

Seminole Wekiva Trail: This scenic urban trail is located in Altamonte Springs between roads SR 434 and SR 436. The path is paved, smooth, and about 2.1 miles long. The area is very peaceful

A great urban paved trail, Seminole Wekiva Trail, Altamonte Springs

and surrounded by lush vegetation. On the trail you feel far away from civilization, although it is all around you. One of the best places to access the trail is the Seminole County Softball Complex, located at the west end of North Street off Douglas Avenue. Here you will find free parking, water, restrooms, picnic tables, grass fields, and a trail map. The access to the trail is behind the parking lot to the right of the park entrance. From this entry point you can run south toward the end of the trail at the San Sebastian Trailhead and back for a 3.2-mile loop, or you can run the entire trail and back to where you started for a 4.2-mile run.

The other great place to access the trail is from Sanlando Park located at the corner of West Highland Street and Laura Avenue. Here you will find parking, restrooms, water, a playground, tennis courts, a jogging area, and picnic tables. The trail access is to the left of the park entrance between the tennis courts and the office building. The Sanlando Trailhead is about the half point of the trail. From here you can run to the San Sebastian area and back for a 2.2-mile run, or to the opposite end for a two-mile loop. This beautiful, scenic trail is definitely one of my favorites. Lots of bikers, skaters, and runners use this trail, so remember to be cautious.

Turkey Lake Park: This beautiful city park, located along the shores of Turkey Lake in southwest Orlando, is a popular running spot among the local community. There are several nature trails totaling about seven miles plus a three-mile bike path. The park has restrooms, water, picnic tables, camping areas, a swimming pool, a playground, a fishing pier, plenty of shaded areas, and year-round outdoor activities. A small fee is required to get in the park. This is a great place to bring the family and let them enjoy the park while you run some of the trails. The entrance to Turkey Lake Park is on Hiawassee Road just north of the Florida Turnpike. The park is located about two miles northwest of Universal Studios.

Waterfront Park: This park is located on beautiful Lake Minneola in hilly Clermont (off SR 50 about twenty-two miles west of downtown Orlando). Several popular triathlons and road races are held at this park. This is a good access point to the seven-mile loop around Lake Minneola. From the park you can also run on the scenic trail between Clermont and the town of Minneola. The paved trail is about 3.5 miles long end-to-end. For a nice run, head east on the trail towards Minneola and return back to the park. This loop is about 6 miles. The trailhead in Clermont is located a few blocks west of Waterfront Park on 8th street and Minneola Street. Waterfront Park has restrooms, water, a playground, and plenty of parking. A small parking fee is required. The entrance to the park is on East Avenue and Palm Street.

West Orange Trail: This is a scenic multi-purpose trail that runs through several communities along the southeastern edge of Lake Apopka in Orange County (about twelve miles west of Orlando on SR 50). The paved trail is about twenty-two miles long and goes from County Line Station in Killarney to Welch Road in Apopka. Although the trail has multiple access points along the way, a great place to start is Chapin Station Park in Winter Garden. The park is located at the intersection of West Crown Point Road and Crown Point Cross Road. The entrance to the park is on Crown Point Cross Road, about a hundred yards west of the intersection. Here you will find free parking, lots of shade and grassy areas, restrooms, water, maps, a playground, picnic tables, and the trail information office.

In this area, the West Orange Trail path runs parallel to West Crown Point Road. From Chapin Station Park, the trail goes for about seven miles west to its start at County Line Station and about fifteen miles in the other direction to its end north of downtown Apopka. To plan your run, check the signs posted by the trail access showing the mileage between the stations. In any case, there are mile-markers at every mile along the trail. For a short run head west towards the Winter Garden Station and back to Chapin Station. This loop is about 3.8 miles. Remember to bring water if you plan on going for a long run. The West Orange Trail is very popular. Runners share the trail with bikers, skaters, and hikers, so use caution. The trail is open daily from sunrise to sunset.

Winter Park Historic District: This historic and picturesque downtown district is filled with restaurants, stylish shops, parks, and activity. From here it is easy to run into any of the surrounding neigh-borhoods and circle around one of the many lakes nearby. The area is reminiscent of a classic American town with its beautiful homes, cobblestone streets, tree-lined sidewalks, and well-groomed green

Historic Park Avenue, Winter Park

areas. A convenient place to find parking is on Park Avenue along Central Park.

For a great run with lots of turns and beautiful sights, start from the northeast corner of Park Avenue and Welbourne Avenue, across from Central Park, and head north on Park Avenue. Go past Morse Boulevard, and continue straight on Park Avenue for several blocks (half a mile). Use the sidewalk. Turn right on Webster Avenue, and continue past Interlachen Avenue. Turn left on Georgia Avenue, and then make a right on Palmer Avenue. Watch for cars when crossing the small streets. Stay on Palmer Avenue for about two blocks, and turn left on Alabama Drive. This shaded street winds around the eastern edge of Lake Maitland. Continue on Alabama Drive past the small park on the lake side (Azalea Park). Turn left on Via Tuscany, and then go right on Via Lugano. Stay on Via Lugano, and turn right on Temple Drive. Here the sidewalk is on the left side of the street. Continue straight. You will see Lake Knowles on the left side of Temple Drive. Turn right on Via Capri, and one block up turn left on Via Tuscany. Make a right on Alabama Drive. Stay on Alabama Drive until Palmer Avenue. Turn right on Palmer Avenue and left on

Georgia Avenue. Make a right on Webster Avenue, and about half a block further turn left on Interlachen Avenue. Continue on Interlachen Avenue for several blocks. Go past Swoope Avenue, Canton Avenue, and Morse Boulevard. Turn right on Welbourne Avenue, and continue straight until you get to Park Avenue where you started. This loop is about 4.4 miles. This area is a popular running spot among locals, and this scenic run is definitely high on my list.. The best time to run is during off-peak hours.

BEST LOCAL RACES

Walt Disney World Marathon: This famous event is held in early January at the Walt Disney World resort in Orlando. There are two events: the marathon and the half-marathon. Both races start together and move in and out through the famous theme parks, giving runners a close and magical view of each attraction. The course is flat and fast with many turns and twists Thousands of spectators line up along the parks accompanied by live bands and Disney "celebrities."

In addition to the races, a runner's expo is held at Disney's Wide World of Sports Complex where you can get information on running, attend fitness seminars, and find good deals on running gear. Following the events, the awards celebration begins with great food, refreshments, and entertainment for all runners. Finishers from each race are given a commemorative medal. The WDW marathon and half-marathon have become extremely popular in recent years, and they attract thousands of runners from all over the world. If you decide to enter one of these events, send your entry in early since both races allow only a limited number of runners. This event offers the unique opportunity to run through the world's most famous theme attractions—a world-class event in a world-class venue that you won't easily forget.

Real Florida 5K: This unique run is held in January at the Wekiwa Springs State Park in Apopka. The 5K course is scenic and loops through the woods of the park. An awards party with food and refreshments follows the run. Only a limited number of runners are allowed in this event due to the width of the trails and available parking. Wekiwa Springs State Park's entrance is located off Wekiva Springs Road about 5 miles west of I-4. This is a great race in a beautiful natural surrounding.

Park Avenue 5K: This event is held in mid-January in downtown Winter Park. The 5K starts at Central Park on trendy Park Avenue and loops around this charming area. A kids' run follows the 5K. After the events there is an awards party with plenty of food, refreshments and fun for everyone. This popular race attracts over a thousand runners each year. This is definitively a great event held in one of the most beautiful neighborhoods of the Orlando area. Central Park is located on Park Avenue and New England Avenue.

Lady Track Shack 5K: This classic women-only event is held on a Sunday morning in late January in Winter Park. The 5K race starts and finishes at the lush Mead Botanical Gardens. There is a coed kids' fun run after the 5K. An awards party with food and refreshments follows the races. This popular event attracts more than a thousand runners. The proceeds from this race benefit a women's mammography center at a local hospital. Men can show their support by volunteering on race day or donating to the women's fund.

RDV 5K: This race is held in early February at the RDV Sportsplex in Maitland. There is a 5K and a kids' fun run. This is a popular and fun event. There is an awards celebration after the races with lots of food and drinks. The RDV Sportsplex is located on Maitland Boulevard just west of I-4.

Outback Distance Classic: This popular afternoon event is held in mid-February in downtown Orlando. There are three races: the main 12K, a 3K fun run, and a kids' run. The races start at Lake Eola Park on Central Boulevard. After the runs there is an awards party with excellent food, refreshments, and entertainment for everyone. This 12K race offers the opportunity to run a bit longer than the usual shorter distances, but is not long enough to require a lot of extra training.

Run Around the Pines 5K: This popular event is held in early March in Winter Park. The 5K run starts and finishes at Showalter Field. The course is flat, fast and loops around the scenic Pines neighborhood. A kids' fun run follows the 5K, and a great awards party with plenty of food and refreshments is held after the races. If you are looking for a fast course in a beautiful place consider this event.

Winter Park Road Race: This classic race is held in March in Winter Park. There are three events: the main 10K, a two mile race, and a kids' fun run. All races start and finish on Park Avenue by Central Park in the downtown area. The course is very scenic and meanders through beautiful residential streets lined with big trees and charming homes. After the races there is an awards party with food, refreshments, and lots of fun. This is a popular event and one worth considering.

Run for the Trees 5K: This unique and popular event is held in late April in Winter Park. This 5K is a point-to-point run. The race starts at Showalter Field and finishes in the beautiful tree-canopied Genius Drive area. From this point runners are shuttled back to the starting area. There is a kids' fun run after the 5K. Following the races an awards celebration is held with plenty of food and refreshments at Showalter Field.

Watermelon 5K: This race is traditionally held on the Fourth of July in Winter Park. The 5K run starts and finishes at the beautiful Mead Botanical Gardens. There is a free kids' run after the 5K. A fun awards party follows the races, where you will find cold watermelon slices, food, and refreshments for everyone. This is a popular event and a great way to celebrate our independence day.

I-Drive U-Run 5K: This event is held in late August at the spectacular Xentury City in the Kissimmee area. The 5K course is flat and fast. A kids' fun run follows the 5K. After the events there is an awards party with plenty of food, cold refreshments, and fun for everyone. Xentury City is located a half-mile east of I-4 on US 192.

Autumn Run 5K: This popular race is held in late September in Altamonte Springs. It is a great race to break in the fall season. The 5K run starts at Crane's Roost Park. The course is a bit challenging and requires runners to go up over the interstate and back. There is a kids' run after the 5K. A fun and rewarding awards party with lots of food and refreshments follows the events. Crane's Roost Park is located on Shorecrest Drive and North Lake Boulevard. This is just east of I-4 between Altamonte Avenue (SR 436) and Central Parkway, behind the Altamonte Mall parking lot.

UCF 5-Miler: This event is held in mid-October at the University of Central Florida Campus in Orlando. The five-mile run starts and finishes at the UCF Arena. The course is flat, fast, and winds around the beautiful campus. A kids' fun run follows the five-mile race. After the events there is an awards party with plenty of food and refreshments. The UCF Campus is located east of Winter Park on University Boulevard (CR 436A) and Alafaya Trail (CR 434).

Dick Batchelor 5K Run for the Children: This event is held in late October in downtown Orlando. The 5K starts at Lake Eola Park on Central Boulevard and Rosalind Avenue. A kids' fun run follows the 5K. There is an awards party with food and refreshments after the races. Proceeds from this very popular event benefit a children's program at a local hospital. This is a great opportunity to run in one of the classic Orlando races and support a good cause.

Turkey Trot 5K: This popular event is held on Thanksgiving Day in downtown Orlando. The 5K race starts and finishes at the Church Street Market area. A kids' fun run follows the 5K run. There is an awards party after the races with food, drinks, and special prizes. The proceeds from this event benefit a local senior citizen program. This is a good opportunity to run for those in need and burn a few calories before enjoying the traditional Thanksgiving meal.

OUC Half-Marathon: This traditional event is held in December in Orlando. There are two races: the half-marathon, and a 5K run. Both events start and finish on Church Street. The course is fast and loops through the downtown area past several beautiful lakes. After the races there is an awards party held in the popular Church Street Market area. There are lots of food, refreshments, and giveaway prizes for everyone. This race offers both challenge and fun.

RUNNING CLUBS

Lake Monroe Roadkillers: This is a small but very active running club based in Winter Springs, only nine miles east of Winter Park. www.roadkillers.com.

Orlando Front Runners and Walkers: The OFRW is a member of the International Front Runners organization, a group of gay/lesbian/bisexual runners and walkers. The club is open to everyone and hosts weekly training runs in downtown Orlando. For more information visit their website at www.orlandofrontrunners.org.

Orlando Runners Club: This is one of the oldest running clubs in Florida. The ORC offers weekly training runs and hosts several races throughout the year. A membership fee is required to join. For more information write to: ORC, PO Box 1134, Orlando, FL 32802, or visit their especially nice website, www.orlandorunnersclub.org.

OTHER RESOURCES

City of Orlando Official Website: Offers lots of useful information such as local government offices, news, visitor guide, parks and recreation, maps, and calendar of events to name a few. www.cityoforlando.net.

Orange County Official Website: Here you can find lots of useful information including an interactive Orange County parks and recreation locator map. www.orangecountyfl.net.

***Orlando Sentinel* Online:** A great place to get up-to-the-minute local news, weather, entertainment, sports, and calendar of events. www.orlandosentinel.com.

Orlando/Orange County Convention & Visitors Bureau: Here you can find a well of useful visitor information about the Greater Orlando area. Lodging, dining, entertainment, recreation, and interactive maps are just a few of the topics included in this site. www.orlandoinfo.com.

Track Shack: This running store has been in business since 1977 and is one of the main anchors of the Orlando running community. Track Shack is a major organizer of local races and a great place to get information about the local running scene. The store offers a full line of running shoes and gear. They are located at 1104 N. Mills Avenue in Orlando (only a few blocks north of East Colonial Drive). For more information call (407) 898-1313 or visit www.trackshack.com.

 **LAKELAND AREA**

This unique region of lakes and rolling hills is located about halfway between the two bustling metropolitan areas of Tampa and Orlando. Lakeland, Winter Haven, and Polk City are just a few of the communities in this beautiful area. Here, runners will find many great places to run including beautiful residential neighborhoods, well-preserved historic streets, and the banks of scenic lakes.

The local running community is active and well organized. Several popular races are held throughout the year. The Lakeland area offers not only some of the best natural scenery in Central Florida but the chance to run in a relaxing, small town atmosphere.

BEST PLACES TO RUN

Lake Hollingsworth Trail: Perhaps one of the most scenic places to run in Central Florida, the paved path around Lake Hollingsworth is a very popular place frequented by skaters, walkers, and runners. The trail is beautiful and includes several rolling hills as it winds smoothly along the edge of the lake. From the trail, there is a spectacular panoramic view of the lake and the hilly streets that surround the area.

A great place to find parking and start your run is Lake Hollingsworth Municipal Park, located along the southern portion of the lake on Lake Hollingsworth Drive between Derbyshire Avenue and Buckingham Avenue. From the parking lot, run counterclockwise on the asphalt path. At about 1.5 mile you will pass the Florida

Scenic Lake Hollingsworth Park, Lakeland

Southern College campus on your right. This is the half-point mark of your run. Continue around the lake until you get back to the parking lot where you started. The loop around the lake is about three miles, but this area is so peaceful and beautiful that you may be tempted to do it again for a six-mile run. Another option to add miles to your run is to meander along any of the beautiful residential streets converging into the lake. Most of these are very quiet, and they have steep hills and plenty of shade. Just watch for cars. Lake Hollingsworth is located about a mile and a half southeast of Main Street in downtown Lakeland.

Van Fleet State Trail: This is a scenic multi-purpose rural trail that runs north from SR 33, west of Polk City, to the town of Mabel near SR 50. The twenty-nine-mile asphalt paved trail is shared by bikers, skaters, hikers, and runners. There is also a parallel horse trail. The Polk City south end trailhead is located at the junction of SR 33 and CR 655 (Berkley Road), about six miles northeast of I-4 and two miles west of Polk City (or about twelve miles east of Lakeland). The access to the trailhead is on CR 655, a couple of hundred yards north of the SR 33 overpass. Follow the signs to the trailhead area. You will find free park-

Polk City trail head, Van Fleet State Trail

ing as well as maps and trail information by the small booth next to the trail access. Restrooms and water are available at a small park across the road from the parking area. From the trailhead you can run north as far as you want. Just remember to consider the distance to get back to the starting point. For a relaxed ten-mile run, head north to Dean Still Road and back. For a 20.4-mile long run, go all the way to the Green Pond Road trailhead and back. There are a few mile markers and several shelters with benches along the trail. Remember to bring water if you will be going for a long run. The trail is open from sunrise to sunset. For more information call the park staff at (352) 394-2280 or visit www.dep.state.fl.us/parks/district3/jamesavanfleet.

BEST LOCAL RACES

Rock, Walk & Run: This traditional evening event is held in early January in Winter Haven. The unique 5K course loops around the beautiful Cypress Gardens, which are illuminated with thousands of lights. There is a one-mile kids' run held before the 5K event. Following the races there is a fun awards party with food, refreshments, and rock-and-roll entertainment for everyone. This is a nice event in a beautiful place. Cypress Gardens is located on Lake Summit Drive off Cypress Gardens Boulevard.

Mayfaire Classic 5K: This evening run is held in May during Mother's Day weekend in Lakeland. This popular 5K race is part of the Mayfaire Art Festival and starts at the Lake Mirror Center in downtown. The scenic 5K course has a few hilly spots and loops around two beautiful lakes. After the race there is a great awards party with lots of food, refreshments, free prize drawings, and entertainment for everyone. This is a great event with plenty of fun activities before and after the race.

Labor Day Road Race 8K: This traditional event is held on Labor Day in the town of Davenport. The 8K race starts in front of the Chamber of Commerce building located on Allapaha Avenue. The course is hilly and beautiful. There is a children's fun run after the 8K. An awards party with food and drinks follows the races. Davenport is located about twenty-five miles east of Lakeland.

Lake to Lake Classic Run: This event is held in mid-November in downtown Lakeland. There are three races: a 10K, a 5K, and a one-mile fun run. The runs start and finish at the Lake Mirror Center. The 5K and 10K courses go out and around the historic nearby lakes. The one-mile fun run loops around Lake Mirror. An awards party with lots of food, drinks, and great door prizes follows the races. This classic event is one of the most popular in the Lakeland area.

RUNNING CLUBS

Lakeland Runners Club: This is a well-organized and active running club serving Lakeland, Winter Haven, and other surrounding communities of Polk County. The LRC hosts several races throughout the Lakeland area every year. A membership fee is required to join. For more information write to: LRC, PO Box 1484, Lakeland, FL 33802, or visit www.lakelandrunnersclub.com.

OTHER RESOURCES

City of Lakeland Official Website: It has information about local government, calendar of events, news, and some useful links. www.lakelandgov.net.

Polk County Official Website: Offers lots of official information about Polk County, including local maps and a great interactive visitor guide. www.polk-county.net.

The Ledger **Online:** Full of up-to-date information about the Lakeland area. Get local news, weather, entertainment, sports, and a calendar of events. www.theledger.com.

The News Chief **Online:** Covers the Winter Haven area and offers the latest news and information about this community. www.polkonline.com.

 OCALA AREA

Known as the horse capital of the US and home to Silver Springs, the Ocala area is a fun place to visit and run. Here you will find several parks, nature trails, historic areas, beautiful residential neighborhoods, and many rolling hills along miles of scenic countryside.

The running community is well organized and active. Several popular races and a marathon are held throughout the area. If you are looking for a little change of scenery, Ocala offers a unique natural surrounding and great running opportunities.

BEST PLACES TO RUN

Historic District: Ocala's historic downtown district and the adjacent streets are great places to do a sightseeing run. Known as Brick City, this area is full of red brick buildings, shops, and historic homes. The best way to run is to go east on Silver Springs Boulevard and south into the quiet neighborhoods, or to turn back along oak canopied Fort King Street. You can easily log a few miles circling around these streets. The area is unique with lots of trees, scenic roads, and several rolling hills. Just watch for traffic and use the sidewalks when available.

Jervey Gantt Park: This is a popular city park located on SE 36th Avenue just south of SE 17th Street. Here you will find a 2-mile trail that winds around softball fields and through the wooded section of the park. Many runners train here. Some local runners enter the trail from

A popular running spot, Jervey Gantt Park, Ocala

the YMCA parking lot located behind the northwestern corner of the park, on SE 17th Street. Jervey Gantt Park has multi-sport grass fields, tennis courts, racquetball courts, a track, restrooms, water, and plenty of parking. There are several parking areas, two of which can be accessed from the SE 36th Avenue side. The park is lit at night, and it stays open until 10 P.M. This a great place to run and relax. For a longer run you can venture into the residential neighborhoods surrounding the park or just do a few more loops around the trail.

Santos Trail Area: This is a popular trail area located a few miles south of Ocala. The entrance to the Santos Trailhead, also known as "canal trails," is on SE 80th Street about eighty yards west of US 441. Here you will find a maze of wooded dirt trails totaling several miles. The trails are color coded, and there is a trail map by the parking area. Some of the trails near the front are narrow and used mainly by mountain bikers. One of the best trails for running is Spider Kingdom trail located southwest of the entrance towards the back. The best time to run these trails is weekdays during the day. On weekends you will have to share the trails with lots of bikes. The trailhead area has plenty of free parking, picnic tables, and restrooms, and it is open daily from sunrise to sunset. The Santos Trail area is part of the Cross Florida Greenway, a 110-mile nature trail corridor that traverses the State from the Gulf of Mexico to the St. Johns River.

Withlacoochee State Trail: This is a scenic forty-six-mile multi-purpose trail that runs south from Citrus Springs just west of US 41 to Trilby near US 301. The twelve-foot trail parallels the Withlacoochee River and goes through several towns and part of the Withlacoochee Forest. The trail is paved, beautiful, and very popular with bikers, skaters, hikers, and runners. There are many trailheads along the way complete with facilities, from which you can easily access the trail. From Ocala the closest place to get on the trail is at the northern trailhead in the town of Citrus Springs. This trailhead is located on West Magenta Drive and West Shellbark Drive, just west of US 41 and south of Dunnellon (road CR 484). Just follow the signs to the trail. Here you will find free parking, restrooms, water, picnic tables, and a trail map. For a nice run, head south to the South Citrus Springs trailhead and back. This is about an eight-mile loop. For a longer run just continue south, but remember to consider the distance to get back to the starting point. Bring water along, especially if you will be doing a long run. The Withlacoochee State Trail is a great place to train for longer distances, enjoy the natural scenery, or find some solitude. The trail is open daily from sunrise to sunset. For more information call the park staff at (352) 726-0315 or visit www.dep.state.fl.us/parks/district2/withlacoocheetrail.

BEST LOCAL RACES

Ocala Marathon: Held in early February in Ocala, this is one of Florida's most beautiful marathons. There are two events: the marathon and a half-marathon. Both races start and finish at the Paddock Mall located on SW College Road (SR 200) about a mile east of I-75. Although the marathon starts first, both runs share the first half of the course. The certified but challenging course has several rolling hills and passes by many gorgeous horse farms along spectacular canopied countryside roads. Water and aid stations are located along the course. The post-race awards party is great fun with lots of food, refreshments, and entertainment for everyone. The Ocala Marathon is a small but well-organized event with one the most scenic marathon courses in the state.

Brick City 5K: This event is held in early March in downtown Ocala. The 5K starts by the Marion County School Board located on SE 3rd Street and SE Tuscawilla Avenue. The course goes out and back through beautiful oak canopied streets in the southeast historic district. An awards party with food and refreshments follows the run. This race gives you the opportunity to run through one of Central Florida's most unique historic areas.

Freedom Run: This popular race is held on the Fourth of July in Ocala. The four-mile run starts and finishes at Veteran's Memorial Park located on Fort King Street and SE 25th Avenue. The somewhat challenging course is out and back through the beautiful tree-lined streets of southeast Ocala. After the race there is an awards party with lots of food, refreshments, and music for everyone. This is a great way to celebrate our Independence Day.

Citrus Road Run: This popular 5K race is held in early August in Citrus Springs. The 5K run starts by the Citrus Springs Middle School. The out and back course goes through a scenic rural and wooded area with a few small hills. An awards party with food and drinks follows the race. This is a great race in a beautiful setting.

Reindeer Run 5K: This traditional evening race is held in early December in downtown Ocala. The 5K run starts at Silver Springs Boulevard (SR 40) and Tuscawilla Avenue. The course is fast and has a thrilling downhill finish. A kids' run follows the 5K. After the races there is a fun awards celebration with plenty of food and refreshments for everyone. This is a very popular event that draws lots of runners and spectators.

RUNNING CLUBS

Citrus Road Runners: This is a small but well-organized running club in Citrus County. The club hosts several races throughout the area. A membership fee is required to join. For more information write to: CRR, PO Box 640903, Beverly Hills, FL 34464 or check their website at: www.citrusroadrunners.org.

Ocala Runners Club: This is a small but active running club serving the Ocala area. The ORC hosts several races throughout the year. For more information write to: ORC, PO Box 5621, Ocala, FL 34478. No club website was available at the time of this publication. For any changes check the RRCA Florida running club website at: www.rrca.org/clubs/data/fl.htm.

OTHER RESOURCES

City of Ocala Official Website: You will find visitor information, calendar of events, weather, and official contact links. www.ocalafl.org.

Marion County Official Website: A good place to find useful official information about this area. www.marioncountyfl.org.

Ocala Sports: A multi-sport store that is a supporter of the Ocala running community and the place to get local race information, Ocala Sports offers a good selection of running shoes and gear. The store is located in the Churchill Square Shopping Center at the corner of SE 17th Street and SE 3rd Avenue. For more information call (352) 690-1851.

Ocala Star-Banner Online: Get the latest news, weather, and events for the area. www.starbanner.com.

Ocala/Marion County Chamber of Commerce Website: Has a lot of information about the local community including lists of attractions, recreation, and calendar of events. www.ocalacc.com.

TAMPA BAY AREA

Tampa, St. Petersburg, and Clearwater are part of one of the largest and most diverse metropolitan areas in Florida. A sightseer's delight, the Tampa Bay area is also a top running destination that boasts excellent year-round climate, outdoor-oriented infrastructure, and beautiful natural surroundings.

Runners here will find a wide variety of places to run including parks, residential neighborhoods, historic areas, scenic waterfront streets, bridges, gorgeous beaches, and some of the best and longest paved trails in Florida.

The Tampa Bay running community is very large and well organized and it has several active running clubs. Many popular races are held during the year, drawing runners from all over the state. With so many running possibilities the Tampa Bay area is sure to have something for you.

BEST PLACES TO RUN

Al Lopez Park: This city park is located in Tampa just north of the Raymond James Stadium. The entrance to the park is on North Himes Avenue across from West New Orleans Avenue, and about half a mile north of Martin Luther King Jr. Boulevard. The park has covered picnic areas, ball fields, a playground, plenty of shade, restrooms, water, parking, and a popular two-mile trail. The paved trail loops around the park past ponds and through woods. The nice thing about this park is that it is centrally located and that you can run as many loops as needed to increase your distance. Al Lopez Park is a favorite local running place and the site of several races every year. The park is open daily from morning to evening.

Bayshore Boulevard Loop: This is one of the best and most popular places to run in Tampa. Bayshore Boulevard is a long scenic road that goes for miles along Hillsborough Bay from the Tampa Convention Center to the historic residential neighborhoods south of downtown. A convenient place to start a run through this area is Ballast Point Park located on Interbay Boulevard. This is a small waterfront park with free parking, picnic tables, a playground, grassy areas, and restroom facilities. The park also has a fishing pier and is adjacent to the Tampa Yacht Club.

For a great run from the park, head right (north) on Interbay Boulevard toward downtown. Use the right-side sidewalk and continue on Interbay Boulevard for a few blocks until it merges onto Bayshore Boulevard. Veer right on Bayshore Boulevard and continue straight. After a few more blocks you will go past Gandy Boulevard

One of Tampa's most popular running spots, Bayshore Boulevard

on the left. Continue on Bayshore Boulevard along the waterfront sidewalk. Here you will see the open bay on one side and a beautiful line of historic homes and condos on the other. Keep going straight on Bayshore Boulevard. You may see other runners and walkers along the way, and if you're lucky you may even get splashed by the small waves crashing over the seawall. After about 2.4 miles from the park you will reach Bay to Bay Boulevard, the halfway point. If you turn here and go back to the park the same way, this loop is about 4.8 miles.

For a longer run, keep going on Bayshore Boulevard past Bay to Bay Boulevard. Continue on Bayshore Boulevard for about two more miles. As you get closer to downtown you will see a small parking lot on the right next to a "pirate ship" by the water. This is the tiny Jose Gasparilla Park. If you turn at this point and head back the same way to the park, this loop is about 9.7 miles. If you continue all the way to the Tampa Convention Center, which is only a few hundred yards north, and across a small bridge to the right, then the entire loop back to Ballast Point Park is about ten miles. Bayshore Boulevard is a favorite running spot for many locals and a must-see place if you find yourself in the Tampa area.

Bayshore Drive Area: This is a scenic area in downtown St. Petersburg. Here you can run along the waterfront streets past historic buildings and the world-famous Pier overlooking beautiful Tampa Bay. Parking is available along the side streets of Bayshore Drive. A good place to start your run is at Demens Landing Park, a park and marina located right on the water across a small bridge on First Avenue South and Bayshore Drive. The park has public parking along the left side.

For a great run from the park, go left (south) on Bayshore Drive. Use the sidewalk. Keep going on Bayshore Drive past the Bayfront Center/Theater. Continue until Bayshore Drive ends on First Street South and make a right. Keep going on First Street South and go past Seventh Avenue South. Here you will go by a small airport on your left. At the corner of First Street South and Eighth Avenue South, turn around and head back the same way. When you get back to Bayshore Drive and First Avenue South, continue north past Demens Landing Park. Stay on Bayshore Drive. Continue straight past Second

Bayshore Drive, downtown St. Petersburg

Avenue North (Pier entrance). Keep going for a few blocks and make a right on Fifth Avenue North. You will see Vinoy Park ahead on the right. Continue straight until you get to Seventh Avenue North. At this point turn around and head towards Fifth Avenue North. When you get back to Fifth Avenue North, go past Bayshore Drive and turn left on Beach Drive. Keep going on Beach Drive for a few blocks. Go past Central Avenue and turn left on First Avenue South. Go straight across Bayshore Drive and Demens Landing Park is right in front. This loop is about 3.6 miles. This is definitely a fun and popular place to run. The best times are weekends and during off-peak business hours.

Clearwater Beach Area: Many locals run along beautiful Clearwater Beach. The beach is wide and flat with plenty of hard-packed sand to run on. A good place to start your beach run is at Pier 60. The pier area is centrally located and serves as an easy reference point. Pier 60 has food concessions, restrooms, water, a playground, metered parking, and easy beach access.

From the pier you can run on the beach in either direction. For

A great place to run, Clearwater Beach

a nice run from the pier, head south for about half a mile to the jetties and turn back. Continue north past the pier until Somerset Street
and then turn back to the pier. This loop is just under 3 miles. For a
longer run keep going north past Somerset Street. The beach continues for more than a mile after Somerset Street. For further reference
there is a sign with mileage distances posted on the south side of the
pier near the water. Pier 60 is also the traditional site of a series of
evening 5K races (Sunsets at Pier 60) held on the beach during the
summer months. Clearwater Beach is definitely a great place to run.
The view is awesome and the beach is first class. Pier 60 is right on
the beach at the west end of Causeway Boulevard after the circle
from the Clearwater Memorial Causeway.

Clearwater Causeway Area: The Clearwater Memorial
Causeway, which connects downtown Clearwater with Clearwater
Beach, is a scenic and popular place to run. A good place to start is
along the waterfront parking area on Drew Street near the cause-
way's drawbridge in Clearwater. This is a half-block south of
Coachman Park and one block west of the public library.

For a great run, go up the bridge ramp towards the beach. Use the right (north) sidewalk. The view of the harbor is awesome. Continue west across the causeway. The causeway has paved paths on both sides of the road. Keep going straight on Causeway Boulevard until you get to Clearwater Beach. Soon you will see a circle where several streets converge. Pier 60 is on the beach side behind the circle. If you turn around by the circle and head back the same way to the start, this loop is about four miles. For a longer run, when you see the circle veer right and go past Poinsettia Avenue. Turn right on Mandalay Avenue and continue straight. Here you will see hotels and lots of shops along both sides. Use the right sidewalk. Go past Baymont Street and past Bay Esplanade. Continue straight on Mandalay Avenue. Go past Somerset Street. A block after Somerset Street you will come to a small circle. This is Acacia Street. Turn around the circle and head back the same way to Clearwater where you started. This loop is about 5.8 miles. This run is a nice way to check out the area.

Flatwoods Park Loop: This is a beautiful rural park located in Tampa. The park's entrance is on the north side of Morris Bridge Road about five miles east of I-75 and Fletcher Avenue. The access to the paved trail is about 1.2 miles from the park's entrance. As you turn into the park go straight past the park station on the right and continue until you see the signs for the trailhead. There is a small parking area and booth by the start of the loop. Restrooms, water, and maps are available at the park station. There are picnic areas and parking throughout the park. The paved loop is about seven miles long and very scenic; no motorized vehicles are allowed on the loop.

For a longer run you can add a few miles by running along the connecting paved roads inside the park. Use caution. If you prefer off-road running, the park has several miles of dirt trails. Flatwoods Park is a very popular place, especially on weekends, when many bikers, skaters, walkers, and runners share the trails. During the week you may want to run with a friend since some parts of the trail are rather isolated. The park is open daily from 7A.M. to sunset. Admission to the park is free; a small donation is suggested. If you are looking for a peaceful place to run away from traffic and noise, this is a great choice.

Fort De Soto Park: This is a very scenic island park located south of Tierra Verde in Pinellas County. The park has about eight miles of paved trails that cover most of the island. In addition to the trails the park has a camping area, boat ramp, fishing piers, a historic fort, picnic shelters, restroom facilities, a swimming center, food concessions, and several miles of pristine beach. The multi-purpose trail begins on the north tip of the island near the boat ramp parking lot and goes around the park paralleling the road. The boat ramp area is located to the right as soon as you cross the small bridge into the island. From this point you can run the entire trail or tailor the distance to your needs.

For a nice run from the boat ramp parking area, follow the trail and veer right (south). Continue on the trail straight until it ends at Anderson Boulevard. Make a right on Anderson Boulevard and continue straight until you get to the historic Fort De Soto. At this point turn around and head back the same way to the start. This loop is a little over six miles. For a longer run, if you go past the fort and follow the trail to its end and then head back to the boat ramp, this loop is about ten miles.

Always use the trail path and watch for traffic at crossings. Fort De Soto Park is a popular spot with bikers, skaters, hikers, and runners. Weekends are some of the busiest days. Also, several road races are held at the park throughout the year. To get to the park from Pinellas Bayway (SR 682) take Pinellas Bayway South (SR 679). Go past Tierra Verde and follow the signs into Fort De Soto Park. There is a toll booth right before the bridge onto the island (Pass Bridge). The park is open daily until sunset. Maps are available at the Camp Office located off the road about a mile from the boat ramp. Fort De Soto Park is a great place to run for miles, undisturbed and inspired by the sound of the wind, the natural surroundings, and the peaceful Gulf vistas.

Lake Park: This is a scenic county park located in north Tampa. The entrance to the park is on North Dale Mabry Highway about 4.1 miles north of Fletcher Avenue and about half a mile south of Van Dyke Road. The park has several marked dirt trails, picnic areas, beautiful ponds, playgrounds, a BMX track, restrooms, water, and plenty of parking. There are also several connecting paved roads within the park that, when combined with the dirt trails, can add up to an easy two– to three-mile loop. Lake Park is a popular recreation area among local runners. There are usually lots of people enjoying the facilities.

Old Gandy Bridge: Also known as the Friendship Trail Bridge, this popular trail connects Tampa with Pinellas County. It is a wide, paved trail on what used to be the Gandy Bridge before the new, larger bridge was built next to it. To access the trail from the Tampa side go west on Gandy Boulevard (US 92) past Shore Boulevard. The trail access road is on the north side of Gandy Boulevard right before the new bridge. As you approach the bridge veer to the right and exit Gandy Boulevard into the parking area next to the old bridge. Parking is free. There are a few portable restrooms but no water. Remember to bring your own. There are usually a lot of people on the bridge—bikers, skaters, walkers, and runners— so use caution. The bridge trail is basically a straight 2.6 mile run across the open Tampa Bay waters. There is a steep section of the bridge that allows for a great hill workout, and the view along the way is spectacular. The full out and back loop is 5.2 miles. Parking is also available on the Pinellas side of the trail on the north side of the new bridge. The trail has lights and park rangers are usually on site. If you are looking for a unique running experience, the Friendship Trail Bridge is just that kind of place.

Pinellas Trail: This is a beautiful and tremendously popular urban trail on Pinellas County. The paved trail stretches for thirty-four miles along a green space corridor from Tarpon Springs to 34th Street South in St. Petersburg. The trail can be accessed from many points, since there are dozens of designated trailheads along its length. Some of the trailheads have parking and restrooms available. The north end trailhead is located on highway US 19 about a block north of Live Oak Street in Tarpon Springs. The south end trailhead is located at 34th Street South right across from Gibbs High School, and between Fairfield Avenue and 8th Avenue South. Free parking is available a block before the end of the trail, at 37th Street South between Fairfield Avenue and 8th Avenue South.

One of the best trailheads to get in the trail is Taylor Park in Largo. Here you will find plenty of parking, restroom facilities, water

Famous Pinellas Trail

fountains, picnic areas, a playground, a small lake, lots of shaded grounds, and a 1.8 mile jogging trail. Taylor Park is located on 8th Avenue SW about two blocks west of Clearwater-Largo Road in a beautiful residential area of Largo. The trailhead area is located near the park's 8th Avenue entrance to the left and behind the playground area. Follow the signs to the Pinellas Trail access. Trail maps and information are displayed by the trail entrance. From Taylor Park you can run on the Pinellas Trail for many miles in either direction. For an easy run, go south (right) on the trail. Continue past Ulmerton Road. Keep going until you get to Walsingham Road. At this point turn around and head back to Taylor Park where you started. This loop is about four miles. For a longer run, continue south to 102nd Avenue and then turn back to Taylor Park. This loop is about 6 miles.

The Pinellas Trail is open during daylight hours and is shared by bikers, skaters, hikers, and runners. Although the trail path is smooth, wide, and usually protected, there are many street crossings, so you need to watch for traffic. Also, there are several trail street overpasses that have been built at the busiest intersections. The Pinellas Trail is definitely a one of a kind in Florida and a must-see if you visit the area. The Pinellas Trail is an ongoing project and may continue to expand in the future. The best way to get the latest updates is to call the Pinellas Trail information office at (727) 549-6099 or visit their website at www.pinellascounty.org/park/pinellas_trail.htm.

Suncoast Trail: This is a scenic twenty-nine-mile recreational trail that runs from Lutz Lake Fern Road in Hillsborough County to State Road 50 in Hernando County. The paved trail is twelve feet wide and parallels the Suncoast Parkway, crossing a few rivers and passing through several wildlife areas. The Lutz Lake Fern Road trailhead is located about a hundred yards west of the Suncoast Parkway overpass, and 3.7 miles west of the Dale Mabry Highway (SR 597). The parking area and trailhead access are on the north side of the road. Just follow the signs. Parking is free. Water and a portable restroom are available here. From this point you can run north for as many miles as you want. There are several trailheads along the way. If you run to the closest trailhead at State Road 54 and back, it would be about a four-mile loop. Bikers, skaters, hikers, and runners share the trail so be mindful of others. Also, plan ahead, especially if you will be going for a long run. Bring water and run with a friend if possible. The trail is open every day during daylight hours. The Suncoast Trail is a great place to do a long run or just enjoy the beautiful natural surroundings.

Walsingham Park: This is a big green park located in Largo between Walsingham Road and 102nd Avenue. The area surrounding the park is beautiful and mostly residential. There are several entrances to the park including one on Walsingham Road about a half-block west of 119th Street and two more along 102nd Avenue. The park is very popular and has picnic areas, playgrounds, a lake with a boat ramp, several fields, lots of shade, plenty of parking, and a paved two mile long recreational trail. The park is well designed and spread out so you have lots of space to move around. If you combine the trail with the connecting roads you can get a nice run inside the park. Otherwise, for a longer run there are long sidewalks outside the park along the perimeter which you can combine with a loop through the surrounding residential neighborhoods. Walsingham Park is also a great place to access the Pinellas Trail since the famous trail passes about two blocks east of the park. From

113

the park's Walsingham Road exit make a right and head east on Walsingham Road. Continue past 117th Street. You should see the Pinellas Trail signs soon after.

BEST LOCAL RACES

Gasparilla Distance Classic: This popular race is held in January in downtown Tampa. (For many years the Gasparilla Distance Classic was held in the month of February.) There are two main events: the traditional 15K and a 5K run. The Gasparilla 15K is one of Tampa's landmark events and one of the largest road races in Florida, attracting thousands of runners each year. The race starts and finishes in the downtown area, just a few blocks from the Tampa Convention Center. The course is fast, flat, and goes out and back along scenic Bayshore Boulevard. After the run there is a huge awards party with lots of food, refreshments, giveaway prizes, and entertainment for everyone. In addition to the race, a two-day runner's expo starts the day before the run at the convention center. Here you can get running information, meet other runners, and find good deals on running gear. The Gasparilla Distance Classic is definitely a first-class race. The beautiful course, the runners, and the event organization make this a racing experience you will always remember.

Run with the Nuns: This scenic event is held in January at War Veteran's Memorial Park in St. Petersburg. The 5K course goes along a well-maintained trail in the park. A one-mile fun run follows the 5K event. There is an awards party with food and refreshments after the races. This is a fun event that combines both paved road and cross-country running. War Veteran's Memorial Park is located off Bay Pines Boulevard North overlooking Boca Ciega Bay.

Florida Gulf Beaches Marathon: This scenic marathon is held in January in Clearwater. There are two events: the marathon and a 10K race. The marathon starts at Cleveland Street on Clearwater's waterfront and finishes at nearby Coachman Park. The flat, fast course crosses beautiful open waterways and passes through unique beach communities and residential neighborhoods. Several miles of the Pinellas Trail form part of the course as well. The 10K run starts at Taylor Park in Largo and follows a portion of the marathon course to the finish. A fun awards celebration with lots of food, refreshments, and music follows the marathon. Also, a runner's expo with the latest in running gear is held next to Coachman Park during the weekend of the race. The Gulf Beaches Marathon has quickly become one of the most popular marathons in Florida. If you are looking for a marathon with a spectacular location, great weather, and a fast course, consider this one.

Flatlanders Challenge: This popular run is held in January in the Spring Lake area of Brooksville. There are two events: the main 10K and a 3K fun run. The races start and finish on Old Spring Lake Road off Spring Lake Highway (CR 41). The 10K course is a challenging out-and-back loop through the beautiful and hilly area surrounding Spring Lake. A fun awards party with lots of food and refreshments follows the runs. This is a great race with a tough course—in fact, this 10K is believed to be among the toughest in Florida. Spring Lake is located about thirty-five miles north of Tampa.

Strawberry Classic: This traditional run is held in February in the Temple Terrace area in Tampa. There are two events, the main 10K and a 5K run. Both races start at the corner of Gillette Avenue and Whiteway Drive near the Temple Terrace Recreation Center. The course winds out and back through the beautiful, oak-shaded neighborhoods. After the run, a big awards party follows with lots of food including strawberries, refreshments, and giveaway prizes. The Strawberry Classic is one of Tampa's most popular 10K races and has one of the nicest courses. It is definitely a great event.

Max Bayne Half-Marathon: This popular event is held in February at Fort De Soto Park in St. Petersburg. There are two races: the half-marathon and a 5K. The course is flat, fast, and loops through the park along paved trails and roads. A fun awards party with food and drinks follows the runs. Fort De Soto Park is a beautiful and unique place to run. If you are looking for a great race with a fast course and scenic surroundings, try this one.

St. Patrick's Day Unicorn 5K: This classic run is held in March in Largo. The traditional 5K starts at Largo Central Park located on the corner of East Bay Drive and Seminole Boulevard. The certified course is flat, fast, and loops through the area. A kids' fun run follows the 5K. Following the races there is a lively awards celebration with lots of food and refreshments for everyone. The Unicorn 5K is a very popular race in the area, attracting several hundred runners every year.

Shamrock Classic–St. Patrick's Run: This traditional event is held in March at Sabal Park in Brandon. There are three races: the main 10K, a 5K, and a one-mile fun run. The course is flat, winding, and fast. An Irish style awards party with food, drinks, and music follows the runs. This is a popular race and fun way to enjoy the St. Patrick's celebration and get a good run. Sabal Park is located off Faulkenburg Road and Martin Luther King Jr. Boulevard, just a few blocks east of I-75.

Armadillo Run: This popular event is held in March in downtown Oldsmar. There are three runs: a 5K, a 10K, and a one-mile fun run. The races start at the corner of State Street and Fairfield Street just south of Tampa Road. There is a great awards party after the run with lots of food and drinks for everyone. If you are looking for a fun and enjoyable race try this one.

Beach to Bayou Run: This traditional run is held in April in picturesque Tarpon Springs. There are two events: the 5K race and a one-mile fun run. Both races start at Grand Avenue and Orange Street next to Spring Bayou. The course winds around the scenic bayous of Tarpon Springs. After the runs an entertaining awards party with lots of food and refreshments is held at nearby Craig Park. The Beach to Bayou Run is a very popular event with hundreds of runners participating every year. Proceeds from the run benefit the local hospital.

Seminole Stampede Run: This run is held in April at Walsingham Park in the Largo-Seminole area. There are three events: the main 5K, a 10K, and a one-mile fun run. All races start and finish in the park. The beautiful course winds through the park and around the surrounding area. Following the runs there is a fun awards party with food and refreshments. This is a popular event and it gives you the option to choose between two nice distances.

Dare to Go Bare 5K: This unique clothing-optional race is held in May at the Lake Como Resort in Lutz. There are two events: a 5K run and a 2.5K walk. The 5K course is flat and loops around the Lake Como resort area through the beautiful surrounding orange groves. An interesting awards party with food, refreshments, prizes, and music follows the runs. Several hundred runners enter this race every year, and although this is a very different kind of 5K, it is one you won't easily forget.

Midnight Run: This traditional night event is held in July in Dunedin. There are two races: a 10K and a 3K. Both runs begin right after midnight on Independence Day. The race starts at the Dunedin Causeway and goes across into Honeymoon Island State Recreation Area and back to Causeway Plaza. There are luminaries along the course. After the runs there is an awards party with food, refreshments, and giveaway prizes. Proceeds from the race benefit several community projects. This run is very popular and attracts hundreds of runners. It is a great opportunity to run a unique race and support a good cause.

Paradise Lake 5K: This clothing-optional run is held in November at the Paradise Lakes Resort in Lutz. The 5K course loops through the beautiful Paradise Lakes resort area. A fun awards party with food and refreshments follows the run. Along with the Dare to Go Bare 5K, this unusual 5K race is one of the few events of this kind in Florida.

Times Turkey Trot: This traditional event is held in November on Thanksgiving morning in Clearwater. There are three races: a 5K, a 10K, and a one-mile fun run. All runs start and finish in the area near the Clearwater High School located on Gulf-to-Bay Boulevard and Hercules Avenue. The certified courses loop through the beautiful surrounding neighborhoods. A fun awards party with lots of food and refreshments follows the runs. This is one of the most popular races in the Tampa Bay area and attracts hordes of runners every year. If you are looking for a great Thanksgiving run, this is definitely the one to pick.

RUNNING CLUBS

Brandon Running Association: This is a small but well-established running club based in the Brandon area. The club hosts several running events throughout the year. A membership fee is required to join. For more information write to: Brandon Running Association, PO Box 1564, Brandon, FL 33509, or visit www.brandonrunning.com.

Front Runners Tampa Bay: This is a large running club consisting primarily of gay men and women, both runners and walkers. The club is open to everyone. They host several social and running events throughout the Tampa area. For more information visit their website at www.frontrunners.org/clubs/tampabay.

Red Mule Runners: This is a small but dedicated running club based in the Brooksville area. The club hosts several popular races throughout the year. A membership fee is required to join. For more information write to: Red Mule Runners, PO Box 1724, Brooksville, FL 34605, or visit www.redmulerunners.com.

Tampa Bay Runners: This is a well-established and active running club serving the Tampa area. The TBR offers various weekly group runs and hosts several races throughout the year. A membership fee is required to join. For more information write to: TBR, PO Box 290372, Tampa, FL 33687, or visit www.tampabayrunners.com.

West Florida Y Runners Club: Based in Clearwater, this is the oldest and largest running club in the Tampa Bay area. The WFYRC is very active, offers various weekly group runs, and hosts several popular races throughout the Pinellas County area. A membership fee is required to join. For more information write to: WFYRC, 1005 South Highland Drive, Clearwater, FL 33756, or visit www.runwestflorida.com.

OTHER RESOURCES

City of Clearwater Official Website: News, parks, beaches, maps, and visitors' guide are just a few of the topics covered in this site. www.clearwater-fl.com.

City of St. Petersburg Official Website: Get news, events, maps, entertainment, parks, recreation, tourist information, and many links. The site is easy to navigate and complete. www.stpete.org.

City of Tampa Official Website: Find a well of information including a visitor guide, local attractions, maps, events, news, weather, and links to city services. www.tampagov.net.

Feet First: Located in St. Petersburg, Feet First offers a good selection of running shoes and gear. Its address is: 3487 4th Street N. For more information call (727) 898-1130 or visit www.feetfirststore.com.

Pinellas County Official Website: Get county services information, maps, park listings, and several useful links. www.pinellas-county.org.

Running Center: This running specialty store is located in Tampa. They have a complete selection of running shoes and gear. The staff is very friendly and knowledgeable. They are a great place to get running information. The store is in the Lakeside Center shopping center at 13725 North Dale Mabry Highway (a half-mile north of Fletcher Avenue along the east side of Dale Mabry). For more information call the store at (813) 908-1960.

Sandon Sports: This popular sports store is located in Largo. They offer a fine selection of running shoes and gear. Their address is: 14219 Walsingham Road. For more information call the store at (727) 517-8225.

***St. Petersburg Times* Online:** A very complete site where you can get weather, news, area guides, entertainment, outdoor activities, and a lot more useful information. www.sptimes.com.

St. Petersburg/Clearwater Area Convention & Visitors Bureau: Offers useful information about the St. Petersburg and Clearwater beach area. Events, local attractions, entertainment, and visitors guide are just a few of the topics included. www.floridasbeach.com.

Tampa Bay Beaches Chamber of Commerce: A great resource about the beaches area that offers information about lodging, dining, shopping, attractions, recreation, events, weather, and area maps. www.tampabaybeaches.com.

***Tampa Tribune* Online:** Find the news, weather, entertainment, beach guide, and much more. www.tampatrib.com.

 SARASOTA AREA

Home to some of the most beautiful beaches in Florida, the Sarasota area offers many of the benefits of larger metropolitan areas without the hassles. Here you always have something to do without feeling overwhelmed. There are lots of leisure and cultural options such as theaters, museums, a performing arts center, trendy shopping centers, quaint restaurants, and many outdoor activities. Runners can choose from several places to run including parks, neighborhoods, bridges, scenic paths, and miles of breathtaking beaches.

The running community is very friendly and active. They host several popular races throughout the year. Running in the Sarasota area is always an enjoyable experience.

BEST PLACES TO RUN

Anna Maria Island Area: A popular place to run in Bradenton is Holmes Beach on Anna Maria Island. A good place to start is the parking lot at Manatee County Public Beach. This is located near the west end of Manatee Avenue West (SR 64). The island is very scenic with winding roads, palm trees, quaint cottages, cozy restaurants, and miles of ample white beach. Whether you are interested in doing a long or short distance run, it is not hard to log several miles around this area. Several local running groups meet here on weekends to run. If you enjoy running while exploring new places, there is a lot to see here. Just use the sidewalk when available and watch for traffic.

Ken Thompson Park: This popular waterfront park is located across Sarasota Bay in Lido Key. The park is on Ken Thompson Parkway a few hundred yards east of the Mote Aquarium and right next to the Sarasota Sailing Squadron Club. The park has picnic tables, grassy areas, plenty of parking, and a spectacular view of the bay. Ken Thompson Park is conveniently located so that you can do a number of runs through the area, such as the trendy St. Armands Circle and across the John Ringling Causeway.

For a great run, start from the park and head west on Ken Thompson Parkway. Turn left on John Ringling Parkway. Continue on this road and make sure to use the sidewalk. The area is very scenic. You will go through a residential area and then right along the water. Keep going on John Ringling Parkway straight past Madison Drive. You will see signs for St. Armands Circle. About a block ahead you will come to the famous St. Armands Circle intersection. This is a chic area full of shops, galleries, cafés, and people. Carefully go around the circle and turn back to the park the same way you came. This loop is about 3.6 miles.

For a longer run from the park, go west on Ken Thompson Parkway. Turn left on John Ringling Parkway and continue on this road for a little less than a mile. Turn left on Washington Drive. This is a beautiful residential area. The road will wind around. Make a left on John Ringling Boulevard and continue straight past the condos. Here you will be going east along the waterline. The view is awesome. Keep going until the western side of the John Ringling Causeway. If you turn at this point and run back the same way to the park, this loop is about 5.6 miles. If you go across the John Ringling Causeway and turn back to the park, this loop is 6.6 miles.

Phillippi Estate Park: This is a beautiful waterfront park located off South Tamiami Trail (US 41) in Sarasota. The entrance to the park is on the west side of US 41 just south of the Phillippi Creek Bridge, across from the traffic light at Constitution Boulevard. There are picnic tables, shaded areas, restrooms, water, a gazebo, and plenty of parking. For an easy run through the surrounding neighborhood, start from the parking lot in front of the gazebo and head out towards Tamiami Trail (US 41). Turn right on US 41. Use the sidewalk when available. Go past Southwood Street and veer to the right onto Hollywood Boulevard. Continue straight on Hollywood Boulevard for several blocks. Make a left on Hazelwood Street. Go past Beechwood Avenue and past Elmwood Avenue. Turn left on Glencoe Avenue. After about a block make a left on Crestwood Avenue and continue straight. Go past Beechwood Avenue and turn right back to Hollywood Boulevard. Go past Meadowood Street and veer left to stay on Hollywood Boulevard. Continue straight until you see the park entrance on your left. This loop is about 2.4 miles.

For a longer run from the park you can go south on US 41 to nearby Stickney Point Road and turn right. Continue west on Stickney Point Road across the Intracoastal Waterway until you get to Midnight Pass Road. At this point turn back to the park the same way you came. This loop is about 3.7 miles. A third option is to make a right on Midnight Pass Road instead of turning back. Keep going straight and turn left on Beach Road. Once on Beach Road, the Siesta Key Beach Pavilion is only a couple of blocks ahead on your left side. If you run to this point and back to the park, this expanded loop is about 7.1 miles.

Popular Siesta Key Beach, Sarasota

Siesta Key Beach: A very beautiful place to run is Siesta Key Beach, located off Beach Road in Siesta Key. Here you will find a beach pavilion, playgrounds, plenty of parking, and beach access. The pavilion area has food vendors, picnic tables, water, restrooms, open showers, and gazebos. The beach is almost flat and very wide. The sand is white, fine, and packed. The view of the beach and Gulf waters is awesome.

From the pavilion you can run on the beach for several miles in either direction. To the south wall and back is about 3.7 miles. To the north wall and back is about 2.3 miles. Siesta Key Beach is rated among the best beaches in the world. No wonder that this is one of the most popular places to run in Sarasota. It is also a preferred spot for watching the sunset. Many people flock here in the early evening to see the sun disappear in the horizon. The scene is just out of a movie. This is definitely one of my favorite locations in Florida. A must-see if you are in the area. Make sure to bring your camera.

Siesta Key Loop: A scenic place to run is the loop around Siesta Key. This is a great alternative to the beach. Start from the parking lot by the Siesta Key Beach Pavilion. Go left (north) on Beach Road. Use the left sidewalk. Continue straight on Beach Road. You will go along a beautiful area of exotic palm trees, inns, condos, and houses. After about a mile the road will veer right and change its name to Ocean Boulevard. Here you will enter the business district and see lots of quaint shops and restaurants. Continue straight on Ocean Boulevard. Go past Avenida Milano. Keep going for about another mile until Ocean Boulevard ends at Higel Avenue. At this point turn right and then left immediately on Mangrove Point Road. Make a right on Midnight Pass Road. Use the sidewalk and watch when crossing. Continue on Midnight Pass Road for almost two miles until you come to the merging intersection of Midnight Pass Road with Beach Road. At this point make a right onto Beach Road. Watch for traffic. Continue on Beach Road for a couple of blocks. The entrance to the Siesta Key Beach Pavilion area will be on your left. This loop is about 4.3 miles.

BEST LOCAL RACES

Sarasota Bay 5K: This event is held in February in downtown Sarasota. The 5K starts and finishes at the Van Wezel Center parking lot. The course is very fast and loops along the spectacular Sarasota Bay and through the beautiful downtown streets. A one-mile fun run follows the 5K. After the races there is an awards party with food, drinks, and lots of fun for everyone. Proceeds from this event benefit a local breast cancer program. This race has a great course and a good cause. It has become one the most popular events in the area, attracting hundreds of runners every year.

Run for the Turtles: This popular 5K race is held in early March at the Siesta Key Public Beach in Sarasota. The 5K starts by the Siesta Key Beach Pavilion and goes south and back along the beautiful beach. A one-mile fun run precedes the 5K race. After the races there is an awards party with lots of food, refreshments, and giveaway prizes. Proceeds from the event benefit the local sea turtle conservation program. This is a great race in one of the most beautiful beaches in the state.

Run for Runaways 5K: This run is held in March in downtown Bradenton. There are two events: a 5K race and a one-mile fun run. Both start at the Twin Dolphins Marina. The 5K course goes out to the Palmetto area and back across the beautiful Manatee River. An awards party with food, drinks, and prizes follows the race. Proceeds from this event benefit a local youth program. This is a popular run in Bradenton.

Shark's Tooth 5K Run: This event is held in August in Venice. The 5K race starts at the beachfront Service Club Park on South Harbor Drive and goes out and back on the road. A fun awards party with food and drinks follows the run. The Venice Beach area is beautiful, and it is also known as the shark's tooth capital of the world because of the fossilized shark's teeth that wash onto its shores. If you are looking for a nice race in a special place, give this one a try. You may even get lucky and go home with a shark's tooth.

Bill's Beer Run: This traditional race is held in late October in beautiful Casey Key, just north of the Venice Inlet. There are two events: the main five-miler and a one-mile fun run. The five mile race starts at North Jetty Park on South Casey Key Road and goes out and back on the road. The course is flat, fast, and scenic along the water. After the race there is a great awards party with lots of food, refreshments, free beer, and fun for everyone. The Bill's Beer Run is one of the oldest and most popular road races in the Sarasota area.

RUNNING CLUBS

Bradenton Runners Club: This is a small but active running club based in the Bradenton area. The BRC hosts several races throughout the year and offers weekly training runs. A membership fee is required to join. For more information write to: BRC, PO Box 1606, Bradenton, FL 34206, or visit www.bradentonrunnersclub.com.

Manasota Track Club: This is a well-established and relatively large running club serving Sarasota and Manatee Counties. The MTC offers various weekly group runs and hosts several popular races throughout the area. A membership fee is required to join. For more information write to: MTC, PO Box 5696, Sarasota, FL 34277, or visit www.manasotatrackclub.org.

OTHER RESOURCES

City of Sarasota Official Website: Find official city services and tourist information. www.ci.sarasota.fl.us.

***Herald Tribune* Online:** This is a very complete site where you can get local news, weather, entertainment, a calendar of events, and visitor information. www.heraldtribune.com.

Manatee County Official Website: Find information about the Bradenton area including parks and recreation, visitor links, and calendar of events. www.co.manatee.fl.us.

Sarasota Convention & Visitors Bureau: Offers lots of useful information about the Sarasota area. Accommodations, things to do, visitors' guide, maps, and calendar of events are just a few of the topics included in this site. www.sarasotafl.org.

Sarasota County Official Website: This is a great place to get information about local services, parks and recreation, area events, and weather. www.co.sarasota.fl.us.

SOUTH FLORIDA

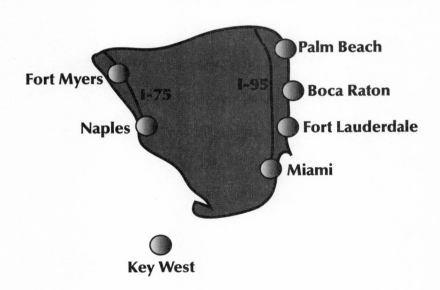

Fort Myers

I-75

Naples

I-95

Palm Beach

Boca Raton

Fort Lauderdale

Miami

Key West

South Florida, known for its green ocean waters and international appeal, is the state's most densely populated region, with millions of people living along its popular eastern coast from West Palm Beach to Miami. The landscape of South Florida is flat and sandy on both coasts, and swampy across the huge Everglades in the middle. Palm trees, cypress trees, and exotic vegetation are typical sights throughout this semi-tropical region. As expected, South Florida's weather is one of the great attractions of this area, especially for snowbirds from the north. Winters are mild and dry with low temperatures in the high 50°s which rarely fall below that. Spring and fall are relatively short seasons, but very pleasant. Summers, although long and humid, are generally not hotter than in the rest of the state. Ocean breezes and frequent afternoon showers help to cool off the hot summer air.

South Florida's running options are numerous and include state parks, historic streets, city parks, beautiful residential neighborhoods, scenic causeways, famous beaches, and idyllic island resorts, especially along the Gulf Coast. The running scene is very active and features several well-organized clubs and thousands of runners sharing the area's best running spots. Dozens of road races, many of them very popular events, are held throughout the region every year.

Palm Beach, Fort Lauderdale, Miami, Fort Myers, and Naples represent the biggest running centers in South Florida. In the following pages I have included some of the best places to run, best road races, and most useful reference information about each of these running areas.

PALM BEACH AREA

Jupiter, West Palm Beach, Lake Worth, and Boca Raton are just a few of the thriving communities of Palm Beach County. A true world-class vacation destination, the area is big, busy, and spread out. Visitors will benefit from excellent year-round weather, many cultural events, major tourist attractions, plenty of recreational options, and miles of pristine beaches. The best thing is that you can experience all of this while still enjoying the area's small town atmosphere. Runners will find many good places to run, among them beautiful parks, quaint residential neighborhoods, and scenic waterfront areas. The running community is well-organized and active, and several popular road races are held throughout the county.

BEST PLACES TO RUN

Boca's A1A: A scenic place to run in Boca Raton is Ocean Boulevard (A1A). There is a well-maintained paved path that goes for many miles along the west side of A1A. For a great run, start from the intersection of A1A and Palmetto Park Road, across from the South Beach Pavilion Park, and head north on A1A. The path has markers every quarter of a mile. Before you reach the first mile you will see Red Reef Park on the beachside. Keep going straight. After another mile, you will go by the entrance to the Spanish River Park on your left. Continue north past Spanish River Boulevard. Watch for traffic at crossings. If you go all the way to Linton Boulevard in Delray

A beautiful place to run, A1A, Singer Island

Beach and then turn back the same way to Palmetto Park Road, this loop is a little over 12 miles. If you continue past Linton Boulevard to Atlantic Avenue and then head back to Palmetto Park Road, this loop is about 16 miles.

As you can see, this long stretch on A1A allows you to tailor your distance to whatever your running needs may be. Restrooms, water, and paid parking are found at the parks mentioned above. Free parking is available along Palmetto Park Road. This area is very popular with local runners and a must-see for visitors.

Carlin Park: This is a popular oceanfront park located along both sides of A1A in Jupiter. The park is about 0.3 mile south of Indiantown Road. Carlin Park has playground areas, a softball field, tennis courts, a small lake, picnic tables, grassy areas, restrooms, water, plenty of parking, and beach access. There is even a 1.2-mile exercise trail. The park is a great place to start a run along A1A. For a scenic run, start from the park and head south on A1A. Use the left sidewalk. Continue south on A1A. The view along the path is awesome. The colorful beach, the spectacular water, and the beautiful oceanfront road will surely keep you amused as you tread along. Keep going straight until you get to the Juno Beach Pier across from Juno Beach Park. At this point turn around and head back to Carlin Park the same way. This loop is about 5.4 miles.

Downtown Loop: A fun place to run in downtown Boca Raton is along Palmetto Park Road between Federal Highway and A1A. This shopping district is full of quaint shops and restaurants. For a nice loop through the area, start at the northwestern corner of NE 5th Avenue and East Palmetto Park Road. (This is across from Silver Palm Park, located on the south side of East Palmetto Park Road). Go east over the small drawbridge and continue straight on East Palmetto Park Road toward the beach. Turn left on A1A (Ocean Boulevard) and continue north on A1A. Use the sidewalk along the west side of the road. Keep going straight until you get to Spanish River Boulevard (about 2.5 miles). Make a left on Spanish River Boulevard. Continue straight across the Intracoastal Waterway over the small bridge. The view is beautiful. Keep going on Spanish River Boulevard until you get to Federal Highway (US 1) and turn left. Continue straight on Federal Highway. Here you will go by several shopping centers. Watch for traffic at intersections. After about a mile, near NE 20th Street, the road will diverge into two roads. Take the one to the right, which is Federal Highway (main road) and keep going south. Continue on Federal Highway until you get to East Palmetto Park Road. At this point turn left and continue straight on East Palmetto Park Road to NE 5th Avenue where you started. This loop is about 6.8 miles. This is definitely a great way to sightsee through this chic area of Boca Raton.

Dreher Park: This is a beautiful urban park located in West Palm Beach. The park entrance is on Summit Boulevard a few blocks west of Parker Avenue and just before the I-95 overpass. The park is on both sides of Summit Boulevard. On the north side you will find the Palm Beach Zoo and Planetarium as well as several pedestrian paths around landscaped areas. On this side you can get close to a two-mile run along paved paths and inner roads if you start by the zoo and follow the path all the way past the planetarium through the grassy areas and loop back to the zoo. On the south side of the park (across the street from the zoo) there is a popular 1.1 mile loop through the park. There is even a certified 5K course on this side that takes almost three loops to complete. The park has picnic tables, lots of shaded areas, restrooms, water, and free parking. Dreher Park is a centrally located, popular place to run in the area.

Dyer Park: This unique park is located off Haverhill Road in West Palm Beach. The entrance to the park is on Haverhill Road about 1.8 miles north of 45th Street and just south of the Beeline Highway intersection (SR 710). Follow the signs into the park. The park was built over an old landfill so there are several hills (mounds) with steep crushed-shell gravel trails that wind up and down. The gravel trails total a little over three miles. There is also a 3.4 mile equestrian trail and a 4.1 mile paved trail around the park. The park has several additional facilities including softball fields, a playground, soccer fields, basketball courts, picnic areas, restrooms, water, and parking. Dyer Park is very popular with mountain bikers, hikers, and runners. With a variety of trails totaling over seven miles (excluding the equestrian trail), this can be a great running option—especially if you want to add some serious hill workouts to your running. Just watch for bikers on the mounds. The park is open daily from sunrise to sunset.

John Prince Park trails, Lake Worth

John Prince Park: This beautiful regional park is located along the northwestern side of Lake Osborne in the Lake Worth area. The main park entrance is on Congress Avenue just south of the Palm Beach Community College and 6th Avenue. There is another entrance on 6th Avenue about a mile west of I-95. Maps are available at the park office near the 6th Avenue entrance. John Prince Park is a favorite local running spot and the site of several popular races. The park has over five miles of paved trails plus a few more miles of connecting roads within. The area is very green and peaceful, especially along the lakeside. In addition there are many facilities including boat ramps, tennis courts, grass fields, playgrounds, picnic pavilions, camping areas, restrooms, water fountains, a 1.4-mile fitness trail with exercise stations, and plenty of parking. The park is open daily from sunrise to sunset. This is a great place to run in a scenic and natural surrounding.

Juno Beach Park: This small park is located on A1A across from the Juno Beach Pier. The park has free parking, restrooms, open showers, water, and easy beach access. Although the beach is very beautiful and goes for miles in either direction, most locals do not run on it due to its steep incline, and because the packed sand is too soft for running. The best place to run is on A1A. For a nice run from the pier, head north along A1A. Use the ocean side sidewalk. Continue straight on A1A. Just relax and enjoy the view. Go past Carlin Park until the Indiantown Road intersection (left side). At this point turn around and go back to the pier the same way. This loop is about six miles. For a shorter run from the pier, go south on A1A for about a mile until the Donald Ross Road intersection (right side). At this point turn around and head back to the pier. This loop is two miles. For a longer run, you can keep going south on A1A past Donald Ross Road for about another mile and a half until A1A merges with US 1. Make sure to use the sidewalk and watch for traffic. The A1A area is very scenic and luxurious.

Ocean Reef Park: This oceanfront park is located on Ocean Boulevard (A1A), south of John McArthur State Park, in the Singer Island area. The park has beach access, a playground, plenty of shade, picnic areas, restrooms, water, and free parking. Ocean Reef Park is a convenient place to start a scenic run along this beautiful residential island. Use the west sidewalk. From the park you can go north on Ocean Boulevard for over a mile to the start of Singer Island and then run back to the park. A popular run is to go south from the park along Ocean Boulevard. After approximately half a mile the road will start veering right toward Lake Worth (Intracoastal Waterway). Keep going. Go past the small Phil Foster Park on your right and continue straight up the beautiful Riviera Bridge. The view from the bridge is great. As soon as you get to the other end of the bridge (west side) turn around and head back to the park the same way. This loop is about 3.3 miles.

Okeeheelee Park: This is a big and popular regional park located in West Palm Beach. The entrance to the park is on the north side of Forest Hill Boulevard, about 2.8 miles west of Military Trail (SR 809) and just before the Florida Turnpike crossing. The park has many facilities including playground areas, soccer fields, tennis courts, softball fields, a BMX track, volleyball courts, picnic shelters, a nature center, a golf course, restrooms, water fountains, a Parcourse fitness trail, and lots of parking. The park is very beautiful with green landscapes, small lakes, and even a few hilly spots, but the best thing is that there are over six miles of well-maintained paved trails suitable for biking, hiking, and running. There are also several miles of connecting roads within the park. Okeeheelee Park is definitely a great place to run whether you are looking for a safe area to do a long run or just want to jog along in a peaceful and scenic surrounding. Area maps are available at the Nature Center. The park is open daily from sunrise to sunset.

BEST LOCAL RACES

Race for the Cure 5K: This popular run is held in January at the Meyer Amphitheatre/ Centennial Park in West Palm Beach. There are several events: the main women's 5K race, a men's 5K run, several 5K walks, and a family fun run. The 5K race starts and finishes on the street near the park. The course goes out and back on Flagler Drive along the beautiful Intracoastal Waterway. After the runs, there is a moving awards celebration with food and refreshments for everyone. The Race for the Cure 5K is one of the biggest events in the Palm Beach area. Proceeds from the race benefit breast cancer research. Huge numbers of runners show up every year to support this cause and share the fun. If you are looking for a fast race with a scenic course and a great goal, this is your sure bet.

Boca DARE 5K: This traditional race is held in February at Spanish River Park in Boca Raton. The 5K course is fast, scenic, and goes along the ocean on A1A. There is a fun awards party with food and drinks after the run. Proceeds from the event benefit a local community program. This is a popular race in a beautiful place. The entrance to Spanish River Park is located on A1A just south of Spanish River Boulevard.

Terry Fox Run: This popular run is held in March in Boca Raton. The race was previously known as Medathon. The 5K starts and finishes at the Boca Raton Community Hospital on Meadows Road. The course runs out and back through the beautiful Old Floresta historic district. Following the run there is an awards party with food, refreshments, and entertainment for everyone. Proceeds from the race benefit the local hospital. This is a well-organized event offering both challenge and fun.

Shamrock Ten-Miler: This traditional event is held in March at John Prince Park in Lake Worth. There are two races: the main ten-miler and a 5K run. The course is fast and beautiful through the park and surrounding area. After the runs there is an awards party with lots of food, refreshments, and fun for everyone. This popular race is not only one of the oldest runs in the area but it offers the option to run something longer than the usual distances.

Turtle Trot 5K: This event is held in May in Jupiter. The 5K starts and finishes at Carlin Park on A1A. The scenic course goes out and back along the road. A great awards party with lots of food and refreshments follows the run. This is a fun and popular race in the area.

Memorial Day 5M: This popular race is held in May on Memorial Day at the YMCA in Boca Raton. There is a five-mile run, a three-mile race walk, and several shorter distances for youngsters. The five-mile course is beautiful and goes out and back through the surrounding area. After the runs, there is an awards party with lots of food, refreshments, and fun. This is definitely a great race to consider. The event is well organized, family oriented, and one of the oldest five-milers in Florida. The YMCA is located on Palmetto Circle South.

RUNNING CLUBS

Boca Raton Road Runners: This is an active running club based in the Boca Raton area. The BRRR offers weekly training runs and hosts several popular races throughout the year. A membership fee is required to join. For more information write to: BRRR, PO Box 810820, Boca Raton, FL 33481, or visit www.sfrf.org.

Palm Beach Road Runners: This is a small running club based in Palm Beach. The club hosts several running events throughout the surrounding area. A membership fee is required to join. For more information write to: Palm Beach Road Runners, PO Box 14730, North Palm Beach, FL 33408. www.palmbeachroadrunners.com.

OTHER RESOURCES

Palm Beaches Chamber of Commerce Website: Offers lots of information about the Palm Beach County area. Lodging, dining,

135

attractions, recreation, calendar of events, and weather are just a few of the topics covered. www.palmbeaches.com.

City of Boca Raton Official Website: Here you can get useful information about the area including local services, news, recreation, and park listings. www.ci.boca-raton.fl.us.

City of Jupiter Official Website: Here you can find lots of area information such as parks and recreation, a calendar of events, weather, and town services. www.jupiter.fl.us.

City of West Palm Beach Official Website: Here you can find lots of useful information about the area such as news, maps, a calendar of events, park listings, weather, and city services. www.cityofwpb.com.

Palm Beach County Official Website: A good place to find out about parks and recreation, local attractions, things to do, news, weather, and county services. www.co.palm-beach.fl.us.

Palm Beach Post Online: A great place to get the latest information about the area including news, weather, event listings, entertainment, and community activities. www.palmbeachpost.com.

Runner's Edge: This specialty running store is located in Boca Raton. They carry a complete selection of running shoes, clothing, and gear. This can be a good place to get running information about the Boca Raton area. The staff is friendly and the store is located in a small shopping center at 3195 N. Federal Highway (just south of NE 32nd Street). For more information call the store at (561) 361-1950.

Running Sports: This running store located in Juno Beach offers a good selection of running shoes and gear and is a great place to get running information about the West Palm Beach area. The store is in a shopping center at 813 Donald Ross Road (just west of US 1). For more information call the store at (561) 694-8125.

FORT LAUDERDALE AREA

Known as the Venice of America, Greater Fort Lauderdale is one of the most exciting and popular places in Florida. Upscale shopping, sizzling nightlife, trendy art galleries, sophisticated dining, unique attractions, and beautiful natural surroundings are just a few of the qualities that make this area a world-class destination.

Runners here will find many diverse running locations from green parks, residential neighborhoods, and historic streets to miles of scenic oceanfront areas. The local running community is very active and well organized. There are several running clubs throughout the area which host many popular races during the year as well as regular weekly runs. Running in Fort Lauderdale is always a fun experience.

Best Places to Run

Brian Piccolo Park: This is a popular multi-purpose park located on Sheridan Street in Cooper City. The main park entrance is on the north side of Sheridan Street about half a mile east of Palm Avenue. Brian Piccolo Park has many recreational facilities including softball fields, basketball courts, soccer fields, tennis courts, picnic

Run on the world-famous Hollywood Beach Boardwalk

tables, grass areas, playgrounds, a world-class velodrome with an inline skate track, restrooms, water, a paved jogging path, and plenty of parking. The paved trail is over two miles long and loops through the entire park. The trail is accessible from almost anywhere in the park, so all you have to do is start running along the paved path and follow it until you get back to where you started. For a nice three-mile plus run just do two loops on the trail around the outer perimeter of the park. Maps of the park are available by the park office near the main entrance. The park is open daily during daylight hours. A small admission fee is required. This park is not as shaded as others in the area, but it is still a great place to relax and log a few miles undisturbed by traffic.

Hollywood Beach Broadwalk: Located between A1A and the ocean in Hollywood Beach, this is truly a one-of-a-kind place in Florida. Also known as Surf Road, the Broadwalk is a wide asphalt path, off-limits to cars, that stretches for over four miles along the scenic beach. Walkers, bikers, skaters, runners, and beachgoers share this world-class boardwalk. The Broadwalk is very popular with local runners and is the site of a couple of annual races. Because the oceanfront path extends for several miles, it allows you to do a number of different runs depending on your goals.

Although it is easy to run from anywhere along the Broadwalk, a convenient place to start is at North Beach Park on Ocean Drive (A1A) and Sheridan Street. This small waterfront park has picnic tables, restrooms, water fountains, showers, beach access, and plenty of parking (for a small fee). The famous boardwalk extends right behind, between the park and the beach. From this point you can go south for over 2.5 miles and north for about two miles if you go all the way to the Dania Beach Pier.

For a nice run from North Beach Park, run south along the Broadwalk. The boardwalk in this area is very lively with picturesque hotels, shops, and restaurants on one side and the beautiful, palm-shaded beach on the other. Continue straight past the Band Shell at Johnson Street and keep going until Georgia Street. At this point turn around and head back to the park where you started. This out-and-back loop is about four miles. If you want to avoid the big crowd of people on the boardwalk go early in the morning or late in the afternoon. Restrooms, open showers, and water are found along the beach and boardwalk. All public parking in Hollywood Beach requires a small fee, but the rate is cheaper later in the day. The Hollywood Beach Broadwalk is definitely a unique and spectacular area to run. Running here is an amazing experience. This is one of my top five places to run. A must-see if you visit this area.

Markham Park: This is a popular multi-use park located off State Road 84 in Sunrise about ten miles west of Fort Lauderdale. The park is big and beautiful with lots of green areas and recreational facilities. There are picnic shelters, a swimming pool, playgrounds, a model airplane field, a target range, several small lakes, camping areas, tennis courts, restrooms, water, free parking, and more than five miles of dirt trails. Additionally, the park has several paved paths and connecting roads totaling over four miles. Traffic inside the park is slow and the roads seem safe; there is a clearly designated bike lane plus a wide grass buffer area adjacent to the road. This means that you can easily log a four-mile or longer run through the park if you combine it with the off-road trails. If you go on the dirt trails watch out for bikes and avoid peak hours, especially on weekends. Maps of the park are available by the main gate booth and at the park office located to the left of the entrance road.

The entrance to Markham Park is at Weston Road and SR 84 west. This is about two miles west of NW 136th Avenue. State Road 84 in this area parallels highways I-595 and I-75. The park is open daily during daylight hours. A small admission fee is required. This is a great place to bring the family and let them have a good time while you run. Many locals run here.

Ocean Boulevard (A1A): A popular place to run is along Ocean Boulevard (A1A) in Fort Lauderdale. The scenic sidewalk stretches for many miles north to south along the popular beachfront areas. Free parking is available on A1A between Atlantic Boulevard and Sunrise Boulevard. From here you can run north or south along the waterfront path for several miles. For a nice run, start from Sunrise Boulevard and head north along the sidewalk. You will be going parallel to the beach for a while. The view is beautiful. Continue straight until you get to Oakland Park Boulevard. At this point turn around and head back to Sunrise Boulevard. This loop is about 4.2 miles.

For a longer run, continue north past Oakland Park Boulevard until you get to Commercial Boulevard. This area is busier with businesses on both sides. At Commercial Boulevard turn around and go back to where you started. This loop is about 7.4 miles. For a much longer run you can continue north toward the Pompano Beach area and back. This will easily add several more miles to your run. Many locals run sections of this sidewalk between the Pompano Beach area and the 17th Street Causeway in south Fort Lauderdale. This is a great way to run while sightseeing in the world-famous oceanfront area of Fort Lauderdale.

Topeekeegee Yugnee Park: Also known as TY Park, this is a unique park located at North Park Road and Sheridan Street in Hollywood (less than a mile west of I-95). The entrance is on North Park Road just north of Sheridan Street. The park is shaded with lots of trees and has several recreational facilities including picnic tables, playgrounds, a small lake, tennis courts, a campground, a swimming area, restrooms, water, parking, and a well-maintained jogging path. The paved trail is very scenic and loops mainly around the perime-

Beautiful trails at Topeekeegee Yugnee Park, Hollywood

ter of the park. Some areas are very pretty, especially around the lake. The paved path loop is about 2.2 miles, so for a 4-mile plus run just do two loops around the park. The best thing about TY Park is that the jogging path is accessible and doable. You can easily adjust the number of loops according to your goals. Maps are available by the entrance booth. The park is open daily during daylight hours. A small admission fee is required. This is a beautiful place to run.

Tree Tops Park: This is a scenic park located on SW 100th Avenue (Nob Hill Road) in Davie. The park entrance is on the east side of the road about a half-mile north of Orange Drive and 2.5 miles south of I-595. The park's amenities include picnic areas, playgrounds, several nature trails, a couple of small lakes, an equestrian trail, restrooms, water, parking, and a beautiful jogging trail. The paved jogging path starts near the main entrance and meanders through the park past the park office into the Pine Island Ridge area. You can get at least three miles if you run a loop around the entire paved trail. Also, the nature trails total more than a mile of paved and wood-chip paths. You can increase your mileage by running these, but stay off the equestrian trails. Another option is to continue running along the paved sidewalk that goes north and south, parallel to the road outside the park entrance. Maps are available by the entrance booth and at the park office. The park is open daily during daylight hours. A small admission fee is required. Tree Tops Park is a nice place to run a few miles in a relaxed and secluded setting.

BEST LOCAL RACES

Scholarship Run: This event is held in February in Parkland. There are various races, among them a 5K, a 10K, one-mile runs, and kids' dashes. The event starts at Stoneman Douglas High School located at Pine Island Road (Coral Springs Drive) and Holmberg Road. Both courses are fast and beautiful, along tree lined streets through the area. An awards party with plenty of food, refreshments, prizes, and music follows the runs. The proceeds from this event help provide scholarships. This is a fun and scenic race.

St. Paddy's Four-Miler: This traditional run is held in March in Pompano Beach. There are two main events: the four-mile race and a two-mile fun run. The four-miler starts and finishes near the Pompano

Beach Lifeguard Headquarters located on Pompano Beach Boulevard just north of Atlantic Boulevard. The scenic course goes north and back along the ocean on A1A (Ocean Boulevard). An awards party with food and refreshments follows the runs. The St. Paddy's four-miler is a very popular event which attracts several hundred runners every year. This is a great way to run and join the St. Patrick's Day fun.

Imperial Point Race: This popular 5K run is held in late March in Fort Lauderdale. The event starts at the Imperial Point Medical Center located off Federal Highway (US 1), just north of Cypress Creek Road. The beautiful 5K course is an out-and-back loop through the streets of the surrounding neighborhood. A one-mile kids' run follows the 5K. There is an entertaining awards party with lots of food and refreshments after the races. Proceeds from this event benefit patients at the medical center. This is not only a fun and well-organized race, but also one with a good cause.

Run for the Roses 5K: This classic run is held in May at Markham Park in Sunrise, usually during Mother's Day weekend. There is a women's 5K, a men's 5K, and a kids' fun run. The 5K course is fast and consists of a big loop along the roads inside the park. The area is green and beautiful. After the races there is an awards party with lots of food, drinks, and fun for everyone. This is a popular event in the area and a great way to celebrate Mother's Day. Markham Park is located at Weston Road and West State Road 84, just west of 136th Avenue.

July Fourth Classic 5K: This traditional evening run is held in early July at Quiet Waters Park in Deerfield Beach. There are several events including the main 5K, a kids' run, and a K-9 mile. After the races there is a fun awards celebration with lots of food and refreshments for everyone. This is one of the oldest and most popular events in the area. Quiet Waters Park is located off Powerline Road between SW 10th Street and Hillsboro Boulevard (just east of the Florida Turnpike).

Over the Hill and the Young & Restless Fall Fling 5K: This unique run is held in September at the beautiful Trade Winds Park in Coconut Creek. There are several events including a 5K for those forty years old and over, a 5K for those under forty, and a kids' fun run. The 5K course is scenic and loops out and back through the park. A fun awards party with food and drinks follows the runs. This is a popular race and a great way to start the fall season. Trade Winds Park is located on Sample Road just west of the Florida Turnpike.

Run Away from Drugs 5K: This popular run is held in mid-October at the Broadwalk in Hollywood Beach. The 5K race starts and finishes on the boardwalk near the Bandshell at Johnson Street. The course is a fast and beautiful loop along the world-famous Hollywood Broadwalk. After the race there is an awards party with lots of food, refreshments, and fun. The palm-strewn beach, the oceanfront background, and the colorful boardwalk make this race a spectacular experience.

Jingle Bell Jog: This lively 5K race is held in December at the Sawgrass Technology Park in Sunrise. Sawgrass Technology Park is located off North Harrison Parkway (NW 136th Avenue) and just south of Sunrise Boulevard. The 5K course is fast and winds through the adjacent roads. There is a fitness walk and a kids' run in addition to the 5K run. An awards party with lots of food, refreshment, and entertainment follows the races. This is a fun and well-organized event that offers something for the whole family. If you are looking for a great race, add this one to the list.

RUNNING CLUBS

Coral Springs Parkland Road Runners: This is a small running club based in Coral Springs. The club is active and sponsors weekly group runs in the area. For more information write to: Coral Springs Parkland RRC, 4609 N. University Drive, Coral Springs, FL, 33067.

Great Fort Lauderdale Road Runners: Established in 1972, the GFLRRC is one of the oldest and largest running clubs in South Florida. The club is very active, sponsors weekly training runs, and hosts several popular races throughout Broward County. A membership fee is required to join. For more information write to: GFLRRC, PO Box 2512, Fort Lauderdale, FL 33303, or visit www.gflrrc.org.

South Florida Striders: This is an active running club based in the Davie area. The SFS hosts weekly group runs and organizes several races throughout the year. A membership fee is required to join. For more information write to: SFS, PO Box 822233, South Florida, FL 33082, or visit www.sfrf.org.

OTHER RESOURCES

Broward County Official Website: Find park listings, interactive area maps, county services, and visitor information among other useful links. www.co.broward.fl.us.

City of Fort Lauderdale Official Website: Some of the information available here includes: park listings, maps, community events, and city service links. www.ci.ftlaud.fl.us.

City of Hollywood Official Website: Get visitor information, calendar of events, and useful community links. www.hollywood-fl.org.

Greater Fort Lauderdale Convention & Visitors Bureau Website: Here you can find lots of information about the Fort Lauderdale area. Lodging, dining, shopping, local attractions, beaches, and maps are just a few of the topics included in this site. www.sunny.org.

Running Depot: This running store offers a good selection of running shoes and gear, as well as running information about the area. The store is in the Promenade West shopping center at 2233 South University Drive, about 0.3 miles south of I-595 in Fort Lauderdale. For more information call the store at (954) 474-4074.

Running Wild: This is a well-established running store and a major player in the Fort Lauderdale running scene. The friendly staff is a great source of area information. The store carries a full selection of running shoes, clothing, and accessories. They are located in the Federal Plaza shopping center at 5437 North Federal Highway (US 1) in Fort Lauderdale. The store is on the west side of US 1, about two blocks north of Commercial Boulevard and just south of NE 55th Street. For more information call (954) 492-0077 or visit their website at www.runningwild.com.

***Sun Sentinel* Online:** A great place to get up-to-date information about the area including news, weather, entertainment, maps, community calendar, and much more. www.sun-sentinel.com.

MIAMI AND THE KEYS AREA

Miami is a big city with an international flair. Known for its diverse culture, sophisticated arts, restaurants, shopping, and nightlife, this cosmopolitan area is also great for outdoor activities. Its eternal sunshine, tempered by ocean breezes, makes for an ideal running climate year-round. Unique places to run abound and include parks, residential neighborhoods, scenic causeways, beautiful streets, and of course, beaches. The local running community is well organized and active , and it holds regular weekly group runs and many popular races throughout the year.

Because Miami is the natural gateway to the Florida Keys, this section also provides a glimpse of the running scene and available resources along the southernmost tip of Florida.

BEST PLACES TO RUN

Cocoplum Circle Loop: A popular place to run in south Miami is the Cocoplum Circle, located at the convergence of Old Cutler, Cocoplum, and LeJeune Roads. A small public parking lot is available across from the circle just before the tiny LeJeune Road bridge. This is a very beautiful residential area with shaded streets and scenic paths. For a great run, start from the circle and turn right on LeJeune Road. Use the right-side sidewalk. Go over the small bridge and veer right toward Ingram Terrace. Make a right on Edgewater Drive and continue straight. Turn left on Douglas Avenue. After about half a mile, Douglas Avenue will veer right. Continue until Main Highway. Turn right on Main Highway. After two thirds of a mile you will enter the famous Coconut Grove shopping district. Continue until McFarlane Road. At this point turn and go back to the circle the same way you came. This picturesque loop is about 4.8 miles.

For a longer run, turn right on McFarlane Road and continue straight past the small park on the right. The road will wind a little and then merge into Bayshore Drive. Go left on Bayshore Drive and continue straight for a mile until you get to Kennedy Park along the right side. At this point turn around and head back to the circle the same way. This expanded loop is about 7.3 miles. A third alternative is to run from the Cocoplum Circle toward the Parrot Jungle area along Old

Cutler Road and back. This is approximately a six-mile loop.

Coral Gables Loop: One of the most scenic places to run in Miami is the historic area of Coral Gables, a largely residential neighborhood with dozens of charming streets, beautiful homes, and luscious green areas. A convenient place to start a run is by the Coral Gables Public Library located on Segovia Street and Riviera Drive. A small municipal public parking lot is available on Riviera Drive between Segovia Street and University Drive. The free, public parking lot is adjacent to the library parking area and across from a small park. From Segovia Street and Riviera Drive, head north on Segovia Street. Use the sidewalk. Turn left on Anastasia Avenue and go straight for almost a mile until you see the world-famous Biltmore Hotel on your left. Make a right on Columbus Boulevard, away from the hotel. Continue straight on Columbus Boulevard. Go past Coral Way. Watch for traffic. Stay on Columbus Boulevard and make a right on South Greenway Drive. Continue on South Greenway Drive until Granada Boulevard, then turn left. After one block turn left on

Biltmore Hotel, Coral Gables area, Miami

North Greenway Drive and continue straight. Basically you will be looping around the golf course. Stay on North Greenway Drive. Make a left on Castile Avenue. Continue on Castile Avenue and turn right on Columbus Boulevard. Stay on Columbus Boulevard all the way until you see the Biltmore Hotel right in front. Turn left on Anastasia Boulevard and continue straight until Segovia Street. Make a right on Segovia Street and one more block ahead you will see Riviera Drive and the library area. This loop is about 4.4 miles. If you are looking for a unique and memorable run, consider this one.

Kennedy Park: This is a waterfront park located on Bayshore Drive just north of Kirk Street and less than a mile from the Coconut Grove Marina. The park has free parking. From this point you can run north or south along the popular Bayshore Drive. For a great run, head north on Bayshore Drive. Use the right (east) sidewalk. Continue straight on Bayshore Drive. Go past Mercy Hospital. Turn right on Miami Avenue and soon after go right again towards Key Biscayne. Continue straight along the causeway path. Here you will see water on both sides of the

Key Biscayne Causeway, Miami

road. The view of Biscayne Bay is awesome. Keep running east until you see the Rickenbacker Bridge. Go over the bridge to the other end, then turn around and head back to Kennedy Park. This loop is about 7.4 miles. For a longer run, continue straight past the bridge until you get to the Miami Seaquarium. At this point turn around and go back to the park. This loop is about ten miles.

For a shorter run, start from Kennedy Park and go south along Bayshore Drive. Continue straight until Bayshore merges at McFarlane Road. Turn right and go up a little until McFarlane Road ends at Main Highway. Here you will be in the middle of the Coconut Grove district. At this point turn around, and head back to the park. This loop is about three miles. If you are looking for a very scenic place to run, definitely consider this one.

Ocean Drive & Collins Avenue: Miami Beach's many streets and boulevards offer unique places to run. Ocean Drive and Collins Avenue are two very popular areas with many miles of sidewalks and trendy scenery. From Ocean Drive and Eighth Street, which is the heart of the fashionable South Beach area, you can run north along Ocean Drive until 15th Street. At this point, turn left on 15th Street and then right on Collins Avenue. Use the sidewalk. Continue north on Collins Avenue until 21st Street. Turn right on 21st Street towards the beach and enter the beach boardwalk on your left. From here the boardwalk goes north for almost two miles until 46th Street. When you get to the end of the boardwalk turn around and head back the same way to Ocean Drive and Eighth Street. This loop is about 6.5 miles.

For a longer run, when you get back to Ocean Drive continue south past Eighth Street. Go straight until the end of Ocean Drive at South Pointe Drive. At this point turn around and head to Eighth Street. This loop adds another 1.7 miles for a total run of about 8.2 miles.

A scenic alternative to the beach boardwalk is to continue running north on Collins Avenue. The area is very beautiful with palm trees, buildings, and lots of activity. Once you get to 26th Street, Collins Avenue veers west and changes its name to Indian Creek Drive. Here you will see a small canal on your left with condos right up to the waterline. You can keep going all the way to 46th Street and beyond. This would allow you to log a similar distance as on the beach boardwalk. Note that the Miami Beach area is usually crowded with people and traffic, so the best time to run is early in the morning. Always watch for traffic and pedestrians. Metered parking is available throughout.

South Miami Beach: A great place to run on the beach is the South Miami Beach area starting by Pier Park near the jetties. Pier Park is located at the corner of South Pointe Drive and Ocean Drive, about half a block south of First Street. Metered parking is available at Pier Park. From this point you can easily access the beach area and go north for a scenic run. It is best to avoid running near the water since this area is narrow, has softer sand, and a high incline. Instead, the best place to run on the beach is along the packed sand corridor behind the umbrellas and the soft sand. This dry sand path is flat, wide, and especially maintained for foot traffic.

For a nice run from Pier Park, head north along the beach. The view is beautiful, with the green ocean waters, the wide beach, and rows of art deco buildings alongside. After less than a mile you will enter the trendy South Beach district and Lummus Beach Park. Keep going straight. If you run until the end of Lummus Park, which is around 15th Street, and turn back to Pier Park, this loop is about three miles. For a longer run, you can keep going past Lummus Park on the beach for several miles. The beach area is very popular and you will likely see many people walking, jogging, biking, and sun bathing. The best times to run on the beach are early morning and late afternoon, when the sun is more forgiving and there are less people.

Tropical Park: This is a popular and beautiful park located in South Miami. The main entrance is on Bird Road (SW 40th Street) and SW 79th Avenue. This is just west of the Palmetto Expressway (SR 826) and about two miles from Red Road in Coral Gables. The park is big and very green, with lots of shade and small lakes. In addition there are multiple recreational facilities including softball fields, tennis courts, soccer fields, a stadium with a synthetic track, equestrian areas, playgrounds, picnic tables, restrooms, water, plenty of free parking, and three scenic trails. The paved trails loop through the park for a combined distance of about four miles. A trail map is available by the rental office next to the tennis courts area.

From the main park entrance veer right and continue on the road until you see the tennis courts on the left side. The trails are

Tropical Park trail, Miami

accessible from anywhere in the park but starting from behind the rental office, the longest loop is about two miles. For a longer run you can do the two-mile loop and then continue with the 1.8 mile loop for a total combined run of 3.8 miles. Another option for a longer run is to do the same trail loop multiple times or combine it with the connecting roads within the park (two-miles plus). Just watch for cars. Tropical Park is a great place to run in a peaceful and natural setting—plus, it is free. The park is open daily during daylight hours.

BEST LOCAL RACES

Martin Luther King 5K: This traditional run is held in January in the Liberty City area in North Miami. The 5K race starts and finishes by the MLK Metrorail station located at NW 62nd Street and NW 27th Avenue. The course is flat and loops through the surrounding neighborhood streets. A fun awards party with food and refreshments follows the race. Proceeds from the run benefit a local community program. This is a popular event with a good cause.

Half Shell Half-Marathon Run: This popular event is held in late January in Key West. The half-marathon starts and finishes at the Land's End Marina by the Half Shell Raw Bar restaurant. The course is flat, fast, and loops around the entire island past historic landmarks and along the scenic waterfront. Some famous highlights include Hemingway's Home, Old Town streets, and the Southernmost Point of the United States. After the race there is a lively awards party with plenty of food, drinks, and giveaway prizes. Proceeds from the run benefit the local high school track program. This is a great event in a very unique place. If you are looking for an exotic location and a fun race, try this one. If you decide to run, consider making hotel reservations early to get the best rates.

Jungle Jog 5K: This unique race is held in February at the Miami Metrozoo. There are two events: a 5K run and a fun walk. The 5K course is a winding loop inside the beautiful zoo grounds. A colorful awards party with food, refreshments, and fun follows the run. This is a nice event to bring the family and enjoy the day at the zoo with them after the race. Metrozoo is located at SW 152nd Street and SW 124th Avenue.

Calle Ocho 8K Run: This popular evening run is held in early March in Miami as the traditional kick-off for the Calle Ocho ("Eight Street") Latin festival. There are three races: the main 8K, a 5K walk, and a kids' dash. The 8K race starts and finishes at SE First Avenue and Eighth Street in downtown. The course is an out-and-back loop along historic Calle Ocho. Following the race, the fun begins with a lively awards party featuring plenty of food, refreshments, and Latin music. Not only is this one of the oldest races in South Florida but it is also a truly unique event with great ambiance and style. If you are looking for a great run, try this one.

Five-Mile Three Island Run: This classic race is held in March at Treasure Island in the North Bay Village section of Miami. The five-mile race starts by Treasure Island Elementary School on East Treasure Drive. The course is a beautiful out-and-back loop through residential streets of Treasure Island, the 79th Street Causeway, Harbor Island, and North Bay Island. A two-mile walk starts right after the five-mile run. An awards party with great food, drinks, and prizes follows the race. This is a popular run with a unique course, scenic waterway vistas, and lots of fun for everyone. Proceeds from the event benefit youth programs in the area.

1040K Run: This unique evening run is held in April in the Coconut Grove area during the traditional income tax week. There are several events including a 10K, a 5K run, and a 5K walk. All start and finish by the Miami City Hall located on South Bayshore Drive and Pan American Drive. The course is a loop through the beautiful Coconut Grove area. Following the races there is a lively awards party with food, drinks, and giveaway prizes. Can you think of a better way to relax after filing your annual taxes?

Seven-Mile Bridge Run: This highly popular race is held in April over the Seven-Mile Bridge in the town of Marathon. The seven-mile race starts on the Marathon side of the bridge at Knight Key and moves west across the famous bridge to Little Duck Key. The view is spectacular with the Atlantic Ocean on one side, the Gulf of Mexico on the other, and both water giants merging below your feet. Upon reaching the other end of the bridge, runners are bused back across for the post-race celebration near the starting area. Awards, food, drinks, music, and plenty of fun are available. This is an awesome race, but it can be hard to get into due to the limited number of runners allowed on the bridge. If you decide to run, make sure to follow the application process carefully and send your entry early.

Tour of the Gables 5K: This popular event is held in May in the historic Coral Gables area. The 5K starts and finishes in front of the world-famous Biltmore Hotel located at Anastasia Avenue and Columbus Boulevard. The beautiful course is flat and fast, and it winds through shaded residential streets. A fun awards party with lots of food, refreshments, and giveaway prizes follows the 5K. Proceeds from the event benefit a local charity. This is definitely a great race and it is held in one of Miami's most scenic neighborhoods.

Twilight 5K: This evening run is held in June in South Miami. The 5K race starts and finishes on SW 58th Avenue and SW 74th Street, or about two blocks south of Sunset Drive. The course is an out-and-back loop through beautiful nearby streets. After the run there is an awards party with food, refreshments, and fun for everyone. The

Twilight 5K is a very popular race which attracts hundreds of runners every year. Proceeds from the event benefit a local children's program. This run offers the opportunity to help a good cause while running through one of Miami's prettiest neighborhoods.

Hemingway Days 5K: This popular evening run is held in July in downtown Key West. The 5K race is part of the traditional Hemingway Days festival. The 5K starts and finishes by the Southernmost Point landmark located on Whitehead Street and the Atlantic Ocean. The course is flat and loops through the picturesque streets of Old Town Key West. An awards party with food, drinks, and much fun follows the race. If you are looking for a great run, this is one you won't easily forget.

Race for the Cure: This popular race is held in October in beautiful downtown Miami. There are three coed events: a 5K run, a 5K walk, and a one-mile fun walk. All events start and finish at Bayfront Park. The course is flat and fast, and it winds through the scenic downtown streets. After the run, there is an inspiring celebration with food, refreshments, special prizes, and awards. Proceeds from the race benefit breast cancer research. The Race for the Cure 5K is one of the biggest events in the Miami area with several thousand runners showing up every year to support this cause and share the experience. If you are looking for a great race with a high goal, try this one. Bayfront Park is located off Biscayne Boulevard along the waterfront line.

Key Biscayne Lighthouse Run: This traditional run is held in November in Key Biscayne in Miami. There are several events including a 10K race, a 5K run, and a 5K walk. All events start and finish by the historic Cape Florida Lighthouse in the Bill Baggs Cape Florida State Recreation Area. The beautiful course goes out and back through residential parts of Key Biscayne and along scenic Cape Florida. An awards party with food and refreshments follows the runs. The Key Biscayne Lighthouse Run is not only a very popular event, but it is also one of South Florida's oldest races. If you are looking for an invigorating experience this race offers a unique course, awesome vistas of Biscayne Bay, much fun, and the option of running one of two great distances.

RUNNING CLUBS

Key West Southernmost Runners Club: This is Florida's southernmost running club, covering the area from Marathon to Key West. The KWSRC is active and organized. Regular group runs and road races are hosted throughout the year. A membership fee is required to join. For more information write to: Southernmost Runners Club, PO Box 5923, Key West, FL 33045, or visit www.southernmostrunners.com

Miami Runners Club: This is a large and well-established running club serving Greater Miami. The MRC offers weekly training runs and hosts several popular races throughout the area. A membership fee is required to join. For more information write to: MRC, 8720 North Kendall Drive Suite 206, Miami, FL 33176, or visit www.miamirunnersclub.com.

OTHER RESOURCES

City of Miami Official Website: Get visitor information, weather forecasts, calendar of events, parks and recreation, and useful city service links. www.ci.miami.fl.us.

Dade County Official Website: Here you can find visitor information, community news, park listings, and county services. www.miamidade.gov.

Discover Key West: This is a great website with lots of information about Key West. Weather, city maps, calendar of events, lodging, entertainment, visitor guide, and several useful links are available here. www.key-west.com.

FootWorks: This popular running store has been one of the major players in the Miami running scene for over two decades. The staff is very friendly and knowledgeable of the area. The store carries a complete selection of running shoes, clothing, and gear. They also host several weekly group runs. Footworks is located at 5724 Sunset Drive in South Miami. The store is on the southern side of Sunset Drive (SW 72nd Street), just a few feet from SW 57th Avenue (Red Road). For more information call (305) 667-9322 or visit their website at: www.footworksmiami.com.

Greater Miami Convention & Visitors Bureau: This is a great website with lots of useful information about the Miami area. Visitor guides, maps, calendar of events, lodging, dining, and local attractions are just a few of the topics included in this site. www.miamiandbeaches.com.

Key West Chamber of Commerce: This website offers visitor information, calendar of events, local weather, and community news. www.keywestchamber.org.

Key West Citizen Online: A very good source of information about Key West and the Florida Keys. News, weather, entertainment, and visitor guides are some of the topics covered. www.keysnews.com.

***The Miami Herald* Online:** Find useful information such as weather, news, area guides, sports, and much more. Visit www.miami.com/mld/miamiherald.

The Runner's High: This running store offers a good selection of running shoes and gear. This is also a good place to get information about running in the area. They are located at 11209 South Dixie Highway in Pinecrest. For more information call the store at (305) 255-1500 or visit their website at: www.therunnershigh.com.

FORT MYERS AREA

Fort Myers stretches over a wide geographic area of beautiful and lively communities surrounded by water between the Gulf and the Caloosahatchee River. The area is home to many historic landmarks, enjoys an excellent climate, and offers plenty of recreation activities for visitors and runners alike. The area is outdoor-friendly and runners will find many places to run among miles of scenic paths, residential neighborhoods, shaded parks, bridges, and some of the state's most natural beaches. The running community is well organized and hosts several popular races throughout the year. Fort Myers offers a world-class vacation destination with endless leisure options and some great Florida running.

BEST PLACES TO RUN

Centennial Park: This waterfront park is located on Edwards Drive just a few yards east of the Caloosahatchee Bridge and across the street from the Harborside Convention Hall building. The park has water, restrooms, picnic tables, benches, a playground, some shaded areas, and metered parking. This is a convenient place to run through downtown Fort Myers and across the Edison Bridge. Starting from the park, go east on Edwards Drive towards the Edison Bridge. Use the sidewalk closest to the water. Keep going for a few blocks past the yacht club and turn left into the Edison Bridge pedestrian walkway (Fowler Avenue). Continue across the bridge. The Edison Bridge is steep and about a mile long. The view of the Caloosahatchee River is spectacular. When you get to the other side of the bridge (right after the two arms of the bridge merge) turn around and head back to the park the same way. This loop is about three miles. The Centennial Park area is very popular with locals, and some runners combine the bridge loop with running along beautiful McGregor Boulevard nearby. If you are looking for a scenic run with a good hill workout, try this one.

Gasparilla Island Rail Trail: This is a scenic, 6.5-mile-long paved trail located on Gasparilla Island. It is flat and runs the length of the island north to south. The path passes by several interesting areas including beautiful homes, expensive shops, restaurants, and lush semi-tropical vegetation. This popular trail is shared by bikers, skaters, walkers, and runners. Although there is trail access through-out, parking, water, and restrooms are available at the Gasparilla Island State Recreation Area, which is located near the south end of the trail. Parking is also available at the public beach area near the town of Boca Grande. A small toll fee is required to get on Gasparilla Island. The trail is open daily from sunrise to sunset. Gasparilla Island is located just south of the town of Placida, about twenty miles west of Port Charlotte.

Lakes Park: This is a beautiful regional county park located in Fort Myers. The entrance to the park is on Gladiolus Drive about a half-mile west of US 41. There are picnic areas, playgrounds, a kids' train ride, plenty of parking, water, restrooms, nature gardens, scenic lakes, canoe rentals, a swimming beach, and a series of paved trails

Well-maintained trails at Lakes Park, Fort Myers

around the park totaling over 2.5 miles. The trails are mostly shaded and can be accessed from several points. Maps are available by the entrance and throughout the park. The area is very natural and makes you feel far from the bustling activity of the city. Perhaps this is why Lakes Park is a popular local running spot. Although admission to the park is free, parking is not. A small parking fee is required. You have to pay one of the self-service pay-and-display parking meters and display the receipt on your dashboard. This is a great place to bring the family and let them enjoy the amenities while you go for a relaxing run. The park is open daily during daylight hours.

Sanibel Island: Located about twenty miles southwest of downtown Fort Myers, this is a very unique place with scenic, tree-shaded roads, unspoiled pristine beaches, and miles of beautiful paved trails. The trails are a great way to explore the island as they meander through the area along shaded backroads, quaint shopping districts, quiet neighborhoods, and peaceful waterways. Metered parking lots, restrooms, and water are found near all the public beach access entrances. A convenient place to park is the public parking

Quiet trails at
Sanibel Island

lot on Tarpon Bay Road. The entrance to the parking area is located
about 0.8 miles from Periwinkle Way on the east side of Tarpon Bay
Road. From this point the beach access is about two hundred yards
south. Follow the signs. The beach is beautiful and goes for miles in
either direction. Here you can run along the famous beach known as
the "Shell Capital of the World," or you can settle for exploring the
island's scenic paths.

For a relaxing run on the trail, start from the parking lot and
head south on Tarpon Bay Road towards the beach. Turn left on West
Gulf Drive. Here the paved path runs parallel to the north side of the
road. Be aware that after Algiers Lane the name of the road will
change to Casa Ybel Road and the paved trail will switch to the south

side of the street, so you will have to cross the road. Although traffic is slow, be careful. Continue along Casa Ybel Road. When you get to Periwinkle Way, turn left. In this area the trail is very shaded as it winds beneath a canopy of trees. Keep going until Tarpon Bay Road and make a left. Continue straight. The parking lot is less than a mile ahead on your left. This scenic loop is about 4.5 miles.

For a longer run, when you get to Periwinkle Way, instead of making a left, turn right on Periwinkle Way and go east. Continue on Periwinkle Way along the paved path until East Gulf Drive and turn right. Keep going on East Gulf Drive past Beach Road and turn right on Donax Street. Turn left on Periwinkle Way and head straight. Turn left on Tarpon Bay Road all the way back to the parking lot. This expanded route will easily double the mileage of the shorter loop above. Keep in mind that the trails are shared with bikers, skaters, walkers, and runners, so be careful, especially when crossing active roadways. Sanibel Island is definitely an idyllic destination for leisure and running. A must-see place if you are in the area.

Summerlin Road: There is a paved bike path that runs for many miles along Summerlin Road from Colonial Boulevard in central Fort Myers to near the Sanibel Causeway. The sidewalk path starts at the Publix supermarket on Colonial Boulevard and goes south on the right (west) side of Summerlin Road. After Gladiolus Drive the path switches to the left (east) side of the road. Use the path and watch for traffic. For a nice run starting from Colonial Boulevard, head south to College Parkway and turn back to the start. This loop is about six miles. The path has mile markers and is very popular with bikers and runners. The area is beautiful.

BEST LOCAL RACES

Edison Festival of Light 5K: This traditional evening run is held in February in downtown Fort Myers. The 5K run starts near Centennial Park, moves through the downtown streets, and finishes back at the park. The course is flat, fast, and full of spectators. You will feel like a world-class athlete as you cruise through the streets and are cheered on by thousands of people waiting for the light parade that begins after the race. A fun awards party with lots of food, refreshments, door prizes, and music is held at Centennial Park after the run. This is Fort Myers' biggest road race of the year with well over a thousand runners, so sign up early if you decide to run. The Edison Festival of Light 5K is definitely a spectacular race and one you won't easily forget.

Treasure Run: This popular event is held in March in Fort Myers Beach during the annual Shrimp Festival. The 5K race starts at the Key Estero Shopping Center. The course has some challenges, like going out and back over the Matanzas Pass Bridge. After the run there is an awards party with lots of food and refreshments for everyone. For more fun stay for the crafts, great shrimp, and colorful parade held in the beach area throughout the day.

Spring Festival Road Race: This traditional run is held in March in Lehigh Acres. There are two events: a four-mile run and a two-mile walk. Both races start at the Lehigh Towne Centre on Homestead Road. A post-race party with food and refreshments follows the run. Proceeds from the event go to support the running program at the local high school. This is a great event and one of the few four-miler runs in the area.

Koreshan State Park 5K: This cross-country race is held in August at Koreshan State Park in Estero. The 5K starts at the park. An awards party with food and drinks follows the run. Koreshan State Park is located on Corkscrew Road just west of US 41 (Tamiami Trail). This is a fun race in a unique place.

Turkey Trot 5K: This popular race is held in November in Cape Coral. The 5K starts at the Cape Coral Hospital located on Del Prado Boulevard. There is an awards party after the race with food and refreshments. The proceeds from the event benefit a charity.

River Run 5M: This traditional run is held in early December in downtown Fort Myers. There are two events: the main five-miler, and a 5K walk. Both races start at Centennial Park. An awards party with food and drinks follows the runs. This is a fun and popular race.

RUNNING CLUBS

Fort Myers Track Club: This is an active and well-established running club based in the Fort Myers area. The FMTC offers various group training runs and hosts several popular races throughout the area. A membership fee is required to join. For more information write to: FMTC, PO Box 60131, Fort Myers, FL 33906, or visit www.ftmyerstrackclub.com.

OTHER RESOURCES

Fast Feet: This is Fort Myers' only running store. It has a good selection of running shoes and gear. Fast Feet sponsors a weekly group run from the store. It is also a great place to get running information. The store is located in a small shopping center at 1930 Park Meadows Drive (less than a mile north of College Parkway between Summerlin Road and Cleveland Avenue). For more information, call the store at (239) 274-9786.

Fort Myers Beach Chamber of Commerce Website: Maps, weather, lodging, dining, local events, and visitor information are available at this site. www.fortmyersbeach.org.

Fort Myers Chamber of Commerce Website: Here you can get information on attractions, lodging, dining, local events, and shopping plus lots more. www.fortmyers.org.

Lee County Parks Website: This is a good place to get information about Lee County Parks and Recreation. www.leeparks.org.

***News Press* Online:** Offers lots of information about the greater Fort Myers area including weather, news, entertainment, a calendar of events, and visitor guide. www.news-press.com.

 **NAPLES AREA**

Located along the southwestern coast of Florida not far from the Everglades, this semi-tropical city of beach resorts and luxury homes, trendy boutiques and art galleries is a premier vacation destination and a great place to run. Here you will find several parks, beautiful historic areas, shaded residential neighborhoods, and miles of pristine beaches along the Gulf waters. The running community is active and well organized, and it hosts several great races throughout the area, among them the popular Naples Half Marathon. Naples uniquely combines the exotic outdoors with refined living, relaxing leisure activities, and friendly running.

BEST PLACES TO RUN

Cambier Park: One of Naples' most beautiful places is the area surrounding Cambier Park. Located on Eighth Street about half a block south of Fifth Avenue, Cambier Park has water, restrooms, tennis courts, a playground, a gazebo, benches, and several green areas to relax under the shade. Although limited, parking is available around the perimeter of the park. From Cambier Park you can do a number of sightseeing runs through the downtown area. The best time to run is early in the morning to avoid the shopping crowd.

For a short but unique run starting from the park, head north on Eighth Street past Fifth Avenue. Keep going straight until Third Avenue and turn left. The streets are lined with big trees and beautiful homes. Stay on Third Avenue until you get to Gulf Shore Boulevard and make a left. Continue for a couple of blocks and turn left on Fifth Avenue. Here you will pass several blocks of upscale and trendy shops. Use the sidewalk and watch for traffic. Go straight until Eighth Street and turn right. The park will be a few yards ahead on your right. This loop is about 1.6 miles.

To increase the mileage of this run, when you get back to the park continue south and make a right on Eighth Avenue. Stay on Eighth Avenue all the way to Gulf Shore Boulevard and turn right. Keep going until Fifth Avenue and turn right. Here you will get another look at this exclusive street. Continue until Eighth Street and turn right to the park. This expanded loop is about 3.3 miles.

Lowdermilk Park: A very popular place is Lowdermilk Park located on Gulf Shore Boulevard North and Banyan Boulevard. This centrally located park has parking, water, restrooms, picnic tables, a gazebo, playground, plenty of shade, and beach access. From the park you have the option to run south on the beach or on the street along scenic Gulf Shore Boulevard. Many local runners run the street route. For a nice run start from the park and go south along Gulf Shore Boulevard. Use the sidewalk when available. Keep running straight until you get to the Naples Pier at 12th Avenue. At this point turn back to the park. This loop is about 4.2 miles.

For a longer run continue past the pier until Gulf Shore Boulevard ends at 20th Avenue. Make a left at 20th Avenue and a right onto Gordon Drive. Keep going south on Gordon Drive until it

A convenient place to park and run, Lowdermilk Park, Naples

ends at Gordon Point. Turn and head back to the park the same way. This loop is about ten miles.

Marco Island: This is a beautiful community located about fifteen miles south of downtown Naples. Many of the streets on the island are built between canals, which gives the area a very unique look. Although the island is primarily residential there is a public beach and several scenic roads. A convenient place to start your run is the Marco Island Public Library located at the corner of Heathwood Drive and Mistletoe Court. There is a small gazebo park with parking right across the street from the library. Water and restrooms are available at the library.

For an easy run, head south on Heathwood Drive past the library. Continue straight for several blocks. Make a left on Auburndale Avenue. Make another left on Worthington Street. Turn right on Galleon Avenue. Stay on it for a couple of blocks and turn left on Sand Hill Way. The road will wind a little, but continue ahead. Go past the YMCA on your right and turn left on San Marco Road. Use the sidewalk. Continue for a couple of long blocks past the firehouse on your right. Turn left on Heathwood Drive. The library will be about three blocks ahead on your right. This loop is 2.8 miles.

For a longer run, head north from the library area on Heathwood Drive. Go past San Marco Road and continue straight. The road will merge into Bald Eagle Drive. Keep going until you reach Collier Boulevard and turn right. Here you will go by several shopping centers. Continue on Collier Boulevard for several blocks until Barfield Drive. At this point turn back and retrace your way to the library. This out-and-back loop is about 4.8 miles.

Naples Beach Pier: The Municipal Pier is located at the west end of 12th Avenue. This is a good place to go for a nice run on the beach. The white beach is relatively flat and not very wide, so you will have to run close to the water to find hard sand. For a scenic run, go north from the pier. The scenery is beautiful. The peaceful Gulf waters are on one side with a continuous line of tropical palm trees and houses on the other. Keep going until you get to Lowdermilk Park. At this point turn back to the pier. This loop is about 4-miles plus. Keep in mind that there is no shade on the beach, so the best time to run is early morning or early evening. The pier has restrooms and water. Metered parking is available on the adjacent streets near the pier. Although most of the beachfront property is private, the beach itself is not. Public access and parking are available on every block along the beach.

Pelican Bay Area: One of the best places to run in Naples is Pelican Bay Boulevard. A convenient place to find parking is at the Marketplace at Pelican Bay Shopping Center located near the southwestern corner of US 41 (Tamiami Trail) and Vanderbilt Beach Road. From the parking lot go past the Albertsons supermarket toward Vanderbilt Beach Road and turn left along the southwestern sidewalk. Continue on Vanderbilt Beach Road past the hotel and the Public Library. Make a left on Hammock Oak Drive and stay on it until it ends at Pelican Bay Boulevard. Turn right and continue on Pelican Bay Boulevard. Use the sidewalk. Here you have over two and a half miles of shaded path through this beautiful residential area of upscale apartments and homes. Keep going on Pelican Bay Boulevard until Ridgewood Drive, which is the first street after the Philarmonic Center for the Arts. At this point turn around and go back the same way. This scenic loop is about seven miles. If you start from the Vanderbilt Beach Public Library and back this loop is about 6.5 miles.

BEST LOCAL RACES

Naples Half-Marathon: This traditional event is held in January in Naples. The half-marathon race starts in downtown near Cambier Park and loops through Naples' scenic old residential neighborhoods to finish back at Cambier Park. The course is flat, fast, and shaded. After the run there is a colorful awards party with lots of food, refreshments, and giveaway prizes. This is one of the best half-marathons in Florida. The race offers both challenge and fun.

Hope For Children 10K: This popular event is held in March in the Pelican Bay area of Naples. There are two races: the main 10K, and a 5K run/walk. Both runs start and finish at Laurel Oak Drive and loop through the charming Pelican Bay district. The out-and-back course is flat and fast. A post race party follows the runs with lots of giveaway prizes, food, refreshments, and fun for everyone. This is a well-organized event which supports a good cause, since the proceeds go to benefit a children's charity program. If you are looking for a great race this is one you won't easily forget—plus you may even get to run along with some of the running celebrities that are invited every year.

John Clay 5K: This popular event is held in early September in Naples. The 5K race starts and finishes at Lowdermilk Park and loops through the surrounding residential neighborhoods. An awards party with lots of food and refreshments follows the run. This race has traditionally been the area's kick-off to the fall and winter road racing season, offering runners the chance to test their condition after the long summer months.

Naples On The Run 20K: This traditional run is held in September in Naples. The 20K out-and-back course is flat and fast and goes along tree lined streets of Old Naples including beautiful Gordon Drive. After the race there is an awards party with food and drinks for everyone. This is a popular event in the Naples area.

Marco Hill Run: This unique event is held in December in Marco Island. The five-mile race starts at The Estates residential development on Barfield Drive. The course is very challenging and winds relentlessly up and down through the sloping roads in this beautiful community. After the run there is an awards party with food and refreshments for everyone. If you are looking for a race with real hills, this event has them, and plenty. This is a tough race with an unusual course for this part of Florida but definitely a great event.

RUNNING CLUBS

Gulf Coast Runners: This is a well-organized running club based in the Naples area. The GCR offers weekly training runs and hosts several races throughout the year. A membership fee is required to join. For more information write to: GCR, PO Box 8636, Naples, FL 34101, or visit www.gcrunner.org.

OTHER RESOURCES

Naples On The Run: This is Naples' only running store. They carry a complete selection of running shoes and gear. Naples On the Run is a sponsor of the local running community and a great place to get running information. It is located in the Gateway Shopping Center at 2128 9th Street North (corner of Tamiami Trail and Golden Gate Parkway). For more information call the store at (941) 434-9786.

City of Naples Official Website: A good place to find weather, city, and visitor information. www.naplesgov.com.

Naples Area Chamber of Commerce Website: Offers useful information about the local community including a calendar of events, business directory, and a visitor information center. www.napleschamber.org.

Collier County Official Website: Here you can get news, maps, local attractions, parks and recreation, visitor services, a calendar of events, and lots more useful information. www.co.collier.fl.us.

***Naples Daily* News Online:** This is a very informative site. Here you can get local weather, news, a calendar of events, and visitor information. www.naplesnews.com.

Run through upscale Fifth Avenue, Naples

Resources

The internet is a great place to find running information. The following list includes several useful running-related websites. Although accurate at the time of publication, keep in mind that these sites can change or be discontinued at any time without notice.

Websites

Cool Running: This website offers running news, race calendars, race results, and training advice. www.coolrunning.com.

Florida State Parks: This website is maintained by the Florida Department of Environmental Protection. It is a great place to get information about all state parks in Florida. Park descriptions, maps, hours, and much more is available here. www.dep.state.fl.us/parks.

On the Run: This website contains lots of running information including race calendars, results, training articles, and shopping links. www.ontherun.com.

Runner Girl: This is an informative website aimed at women runners. Strength training, nutrition, and running tips are some of the topics covered. www.runnergirl.com.

Organizations

The **American Running Association** hosts a very complete website with a variety of running articles and information. www.americanrunning.org.

The **Road Runners Club of America (RRCA)** is a national organization representing hundreds of road-running clubs in the United States. Their website contains lots of information including the list and contact names of all registered running clubs in Florida. www.rrca.org.

The **United States Track and Field (USATF)** is the governing body for track and field in the United States. Their website has the latest official running news and information for both track and road running. www.usatf.org.

MAGAZINES AND OTHER PUBLICATIONS

Florida Running & Triathlon is a popular running publication for Florida. Race schedules, event results, and news are available at their website, www.flrunning.com.

Runner's World is a monthly running magazine available at most bookstores and newsstands. *Runner's World* offers a free online version of the magazine with useful information about a broad range of running-related topics including women's running, new runner's advice, injury prevention, training tips, and nationwide race schedules. Available at www.runnersworld.com.

Running Times is a monthly running magazine available at bookstores and newsstands. Running news, race schedules, apparel guides, and training advice are a few of the topics featured. www.runningtimes.com.

BIBLIOGRAPHIC REFERENCES

Florida State Parks Guide. Tallahassee, FL: Florida Park Service, Division of Recreation and Parks, 2000.

Herreros, Mauricio. *Simply Running: An Inspirational and Common Sense Guide to Running.* Fayetteville, NC: Old Mountain Press, 1999.

Ohr, Tim. *Florida's Fabulous Trail Guide.* Tampa, FL: World Publications, 2001.

Oswald, Tom. *Bicycling in Florida: The Cyclist's Road and Off-Road Guide.* Sarasota, FL: Pineapple Press, Inc., 1999.

Strutin, Michal. *Florida State Parks: A Complete Recreation Guide.* Seattle, WA: The Mountaineers Books, 2000.

PACE CHART

Minutes/ Mile	5 km	5 miles	10 km
5:00	15:32	25:00	31:04
5:15	16:19	26:15	32:37
5:30	17:05	27:30	34:11
5:45	17:52	28:45	35:44
6:00	18:38	30:00	37:17
6:15	19:25	31:15	38:50
6:30	20:12	32:30	40:23
6:45	20:58	33:45	41:57
7:00	21:45	35:00	43:30
7:15	22:31	36:15	45:03
7:30	23:18	37:30	46:36
7:45	24:05	38:45	48:09
8:00	24:51	40:00	49:43
8:15	25:38	41:15	51:16
8:30	26:24	42:30	52:49
8:45	27:11	43:45	54:22
9:00	27:58	45:00	55:55
9:15	28:44	46:15	57:29
9:30	29:31	47:30	59:02
9:45	30:18	48:45	1:00:35
10:00	31:04	50:00	1:02:08
10:15	31:51	51:15	1:03:42
10:30	32:37	52:30	1:05:15
10:45	33:24	53:45	1:06:48
11:00	34:11	55:00	1:08:21
11:15	34:57	56:15	1:09:54
11:30	35:44	57:30	1:11:27
11:45	36:30	58:45	1:13:01
12:00	37:17	1:00:00	1:14:34
12:15	38:04	1:01:15	1:16:07
12:30	38:50	1:02:30	1:17:40
12:45	39:37	1:03:45	1:19:13
13:00	40:23	1:05:00	1:20:47

Conversions

5 km = 3.107 miles 10 km = 6.214 miles 15 km= 9.321 miles

15 km	Half-Marathon	Marathon
46:36	1:05:33	2:11:06
48:56	1:08:49	2:17:39
51:16	1:12:06	2:24:12
53:36	1:15:23	2:30:45
55:55	1:18:39	2:37:19
58:15	1:21:56	2:43:52
1:00:35	1:25:13	2:50:25
1:02:55	1:28:29	2:56:59
1:05:15	1:31:46	3:03:32
1:07:34	1:35:03	3:10:05
1:09:54	1:38:19	3:16:38
1:12:14	1:41:36	3:23:12
1:14:34	1:44:53	3:29:45
1:16:54	1:48:09	3:36:18
1:19:13	1:51:26	3:42:52
1:21:33	1:54:42	3:49:25
1:23:53	1:57:59	3:55:58
1:26:13	2:01:16	4:02:31
1:28:33	2:04:32	4:09:05
1:30:53	2:07:49	4:15:38
1:33:12	2:11:06	4:22:11
1:35:32	2:14:22	4:28:45
1:37:52	2:17:39	4:35:18
1:40:12	2:20:55	4:41:51
1:42:32	2:24:12	4:48:24
1:44:52	2:27:28	4:54:58
1:47:11	2:30:45	5:01:31
1:49:31	2:34:02	5:08:04
1:51:51	2:37:19	5:14:37
1:54:11	2:40:35	5:21:11
1:56:31	2:43:52	5:27:44
1:58:51	2:47:09	5:34:17
2:01:11	2:50:26	5:40:50

Half-Marathon= 13.109 miles Marathon= 26.219 miles

ROAD RACES BY MONTH

Event Name	Location	Section/Page
Winter Beaches Runs 5M and 10M	Jacksonville Beach	Jacksonville Area, 9
Ortega River Run 5M	Jacksonville	Jacksonville Area, 9
Greater Gainesville 5K	Gainesville	Gainesville Area, 27
Flash 12K	Tallahassee	Tallahassee Area, 36
Mardi Gras 5K	Panama City	Panama City Area, 41
Double Bridge Run	Pensacola	Pensacola Area, 54
Blue Angel Marathon	Pensacola	Pensacola Area, 55
Tiger Dash Run	Melbourne	Space Coast Area, 73
Del Hagin Memorial 15K	Hobe Sound	Treasure Coast Area, 81
Sunrunners 10K	Vero Beach	Treasure Coast Area, 81
RDV 5K	Maitland	Orlando Area, 92
Outback Distance Classic	Orlando	Orlando Area, 92
Ocala Marathon	Ocala	Ocala Area, 102
Strawberry Classic	Tampa	Tampa Bay Area, 115
Max Bayne Half-Marathon	St. Petersburg	Tampa Bay Area, 115
Sarasota Bay 5K	Sarasota	Sarasota Area, 123
Boca DARE 5K	Boca Raton	Palm Beach Area, 134
Scholarship Run	Parkland	Fort Lauderdale Area, 141
Jungle Jog 5K	Miami	Miami Area, 151
Edison Festival of Light 5K	Ft. Myers	Ft. Myers Area, 159

Event Name	Location	Section/Page
Gate River Run 15K	Jacksonville	Jacksonville Area, 9
Twilight Lighthouse 5K	St. Augustine	St. Augustine Area, 18
Springtime 10K	Tallahassee	Tallahassee Area, 36
Sandpiper 5K	Ormond Beach	Daytona Beach Area, 65
Easter Beach Run	Daytona Beach	Daytona Beach Area, 66
Space Walk of Fame 8K	Titusville	Space Coast Area, 73
Run Around the Pines 5K	Winter Park	Orlando Area, 92

Winter Park Road Race	Winter Park	Orlando Area, 92-93
Brick City 5K	Ocala	Ocala Area, 102
St. Patrick's Day Unicorn 5K	Largo	Tampa Bay Area, 115
Shamrock Classic– St. Patrick's Run	Brandon	Tampa Bay Area, 116
Armadillo Run	Oldsmar	Tampa Bay Area, 116
Run for the Turtles	Sarasota	Sarasota Area, 123
Run for Runaways 5K	Bradenton	Sarasota Area, 123
Terry Fox Run	Boca Raton	Palm Beach Area, 135
Shamrock Ten-Miler	Lake Worth	Palm Beach Area, 135
St. Paddy's Four-Miler	Pompano Beach	Fort Lauderdale Area, 141
Imperial Point Race	Ft. Lauderdale	Fort Lauderdale Area, 142
Calle Ocho 8K Run	Miami	Miami Area, 151
Five-Mile Three Island Run	Miami	Miami Area, 151
Treasure Run	Ft. Myers Beach	Fort Myers Area, 160
Spring Festival Road Race	Lehigh Acres	Fort Myers Area, 160
Hope For Children 10K	Naples	Naples Area, 165

APRIL RACES

Event Name	Location	Section/Page
Run to the Sun 8K	Orange Park	Jacksonville Area, 10
Catfish 5K	Crescent City	Palatka Area, 21
Haile Plantation Tri-State Run	Gainesville	Gainesville Area, 27
Palace Saloon 5K	Tallahassee	Tallahassee Area, 36
Trailblazer Run	Ft. Walton Beach	Fort Walton Beach Area, 47
Melbourne Art Festival 5K	Melbourne	Space Coast Area, 73
LOST 7-Miler	Port Mayaca	Treasure Coast Area, 82
Run for the Trees 5K	Winter Park	Orlando Area, 93
Beach to Bayou Run	Tarpon Springs	Tampa Bay Area, 116
Seminole Stampede Run	Largo	Tampa Bay Area, 116
1040K Run	Miami	Miami Area, 152
Seven-Mile Bridge Run	Marathon	Miami Area, 152

Event Name	Location	Section/Page
Shrimp Festival 5K	Fernandina Beach	Jacksonville Area, 10
Memorial Day 5K	Green Cove Springs	Jacksonville Area, 10
Gamble Rogers Folk Festival 10K	St. Augustine	St. Augustine Area, 18
Floyd 4M	Palatka	Palatka Area, 22
Race Judicata 5K	Panama City	Panama City Area, 42
Fiesta Run	Pensacola	Pensacola Area, 55
Race for the Cure 5K	Daytona Beach	Daytona Beach Area, 66
Run for the Pineapple 5K	Sewall's Point	Treasure Coast Area, 82
Mayfaire Classic 5K	Lakeland	Lakeland Area, 98
Dare to Go Bare 5K	Lutz	Tampa Bay Area, 116
Turtle Trot 5K	Jupiter	Palm Beach Area, 135
Memorial Day 5M	Boca Raton	Palm Beach Area, 135
Run for the Roses 5K	Sunrise	Fort Lauderdale Area, 142
Tour of the Gables 5K	Miami	Miami Area, 152

Event Name	Location	Section/Page
Run for the Pies 5K	Jacksonville	Jacksonville Area, 10
Billy Bowlegs 5K	Ft. Walton Beach	Fort Walton Beach Area, 48
Firecracker Ten-Miler	Daytona Beach	Daytona Beach Area, 66
Twilight 5K	Miami	Miami Area, 45

Event Name	Location	Section/Page
Bridge of Lions 5K	St. Augustine	St. Augustine Area, 19
Melon Run 3M	Gainesville	Gainesville Area, 28
Jalapeno 5K	Fort Pierce	Treasure Coast Area, 82
Watermelon 5K	Winter Park	Orlando Area, 93
Freedom Run	Ocala	Ocala Area, 102
Midnight Run	Dunedin	Tampa Bay Area, 117
July Fourth Classic 5K	Deerfield Beach	Fort Lauderdale Area, 153
Hemingway Days 5K	Key West	Miami Area, 153

AUGUST RACES

Event Name	Location	Section/Page
Tour de Pain	Jacksonville	Jacksonville Area, 11
Summer Beach Run 5M	Jacksonville Beach	Jacksonville Area, 11
Tom Brown Bash	Tallahassee	Tallahassee Area, 37
Bushwacker 5K	Pensacola Beach	Pensacola Area, 55
I-Drive U-Run 5K	Orlando	Orlando Area, 93
Citrus Road Run	Citrus Springs	Ocala Area, 102
Shark's Tooth 5K Run	Venice	Sarasota Area, 124
Koreshan State Park 5K	Estero	Fort Myers Area, 160

SEPTEMBER RACES

Event Name	Location	Section/Page
Autumn Fitness 5K	Orange Park	Jacksonville Area, 11
Dog Days Run	Gainesville	Gainesville Area, 28
Run for Sickle Cell	Tallahassee	Tallahassee Area, 37
Midnight Chase 5K	Panama City	Panama City Area, 42
Mid-Bay Bridge Run	Destin	Fort Walton Beach Area, 48
Marine Corps Aviation Association Run	Pensacola	Pensacola Area, 55
Seafood Festival 5K	Pensacola	Pensacola Area, 56
Tomoka Four-Miler	Ormond Beach	Daytona Beach Area, 67
Sandsprit 5K	Stuart	Treasure Coast Area, 82
Autumn Run 5K	Altamonte Springs	Orlando Area, 93
Labor Day Road Race 8K	Davenport	Lakeland Area, 98
Over the Hill and the Young & Restless Fall Fling 5K	Coconut Creek	Fort Lauderdale Area, 142
John Clay 5K	Naples	Naples Area, 165
Naples On The Run 20K	Naples	Naples Area, 165

OCTOBER RACES

Event Name	Location	Section/Page
Micanopy Half-Marathon	Micanopy	Gainesville Area, 28
Women's Distance Festival	Tallahassee	Tallahassee Area, 37
Tricker Trek 10K	Panama City	Panama City Area, 42
Mullet Festival 3M Run	Niceville	Fort Walton Beach Area, 48
McGuire's Sunset Run	Destin	Fort Walton Beach Area, 48
Paint the Towne 5K	Daytona Beach	Daytona Beach Area, 67
Pumpkins in the Park 5K	Cocoa	Space Coast Area, 73
Jungle Jog 5K	Vero Beach	Treasure Coast Area, 82
Halloween 10K	Hobe Sound	Treasure Coast Area, 83
UCF Five-Miler	Orlando	Orlando Area
Dick Batchelor 5K Run for the Children	Orlando	Orlando Area, 94
Bill's Beer Run	Casey Key	Sarasota Area, 124
Run Away from Drugs 5K	Hollywood Beach	Fort Lauderdale Area, 143
Race for the Cure	Miami	Miami Area, 153

NOVEMBER RACES

Event Name	Location	Section/Page
Outback Half-Marathon	Jacksonville	Jacksonville Area, 12
Turkey Trot Run	Tallahassee	Tallahassee Area, 38
Draggin' Tail 18-Mile Run and Relay	Sunny Hills	Panama City Area, 42
Timberlake Run	Ft. Walton Beach	Fort Walton Beach Area, 48
Turkey Trot 5K	Pensacola	Pensacola Area, 56
Paul de Bruyn Memorial Run	Ormond Beach	Daytona Beach Area, 67
Space Coast Classic 15K	Cocoa	Space Coast Area, 74

Space Coast Marathon	Melbourne	Space Coast Area, 74
Dolphin Dash 5K	Vero Beach	Treasure Coast Area, 83
Harbor Branch 5K	Fort Pierce	Treasure Coast Area, 83
Turkey Trot 5K	Orlando	Orlando Area, 94
Lake to Lake Classic Run	Lakeland	Lakeland Area, 98
Paradise Lake 5K	Lutz	Tampa Bay Area, 117
Times Turkey Trot	Clearwater	Tampa Bay Area, 117
Key Biscayne Lighthouse Run	Miami	Miami Area, 153
Turkey Trot 5K	Cape Coral	Fort Myers Area, 160

DECEMBER RACES

Event Name	Location	Section/Page
Jacksonville Marathon	Jacksonville	Jacksonville Area, 12
Jingle Bell Run	Tallahassee	Tallahassee Area, 38
Jack Island Run	Fort Pierce	Treasure Coast Area, 83
OUC Half-Marathon	Orlando	Orlando Area, 94
Reindeer Run 5K	Ocala	Ocala Area, 103
Jingle Bell Jog	Sunrise	Fort Lauderdale Area, 143
River Run 5M	Ft. Myers	Fort Myers Area, 160
Marco Hill Run	Marco Island	Naples Area, 165

If you enjoyed reading this book, check out these other Pineapple Press titles. To request our complete catalog or to place an order, write to Pineapple Press, P.O. Box 3889, Sarasota, Florida 34230, or call 1-800-PINEAPL (746-3275). Or visit our website at www.pineapplepress.com.

52 Great Florida Golf Getaways by Ed Schmidt, Jr. From the white sand bunkers of the Panhandle to the palmetto-framed fairways of Miami, this book offers Florida's best places to tee up—including information on courses, strategies, golf schools, and course architects. ISBN 1-56164-260-6 (pb)

Adventure Sports in Florida by Bruce Hunt. More than a guidebook, this lively chronicle of the author's adventures in high-adrenaline sports schools in Florida puts you in the "hot seat" every time. Includes sky diving, sports car racing, hang gliding, sea kayaking, cavern diving, and more. ISBN 1-56164-095-6 (pb)

Alligator Tales by Kevin M. McCarthy. True and tongue-in-cheek accounts of alligators and the people who have hunted them, been attacked by them, and tried to save them from extinction. Filled with amusing black-and-white photos and punctuated by a full-color section. ISBN 1-56164-158-8 (pb)

Baseball in Florida by Kevin McCarthy. In this comprehensive survey of Florida baseball, you'll meet the heroes who delighted fans of all ages and visit the small-town diamonds and the big-league fields. Among the many useful appendices are lists of minor league sites in Florida, spring training sites and dates, and Florida-born major league players. ISBN 1-56164-097-2 (hb); 1-56164-089-1 (pb)

Bicycling in Florida by Tom Oswald. Divided by region, this book outlines 71 rides including complete directions, maps, and pertinent information. This jam-packed guide also discusses cycling laws and safety issues, and lists names and addresses of area bike associations for each region. ISBN 1-56164-161-8 (pb)

The Exploring Wild Florida series: A set of field guides, each with information on all the parks, preserves, and natural areas in its region, including wildlife to look for and best time of year to visit.

Exploring Wild North Florida by Gil Nelson. From the Suwannee River to the Atlantic shore, and south to include the Ocala National Forest. ISBN 1-56164-091-3 (pb)

Exploring Wild Northwest Florida by Gil Nelson. The Florida Panhandle, from the Perdido River in the west to the Suwannee River in the east. ISBN 1-56164-086-7 (pb)

Exploring Wild South Florida, Third Edition by Susan D. Jewell. From Hobe Sound and Punta Gorda south to include the Keys and the Dry Tortugas. Expanded edition covers Broward, Hendry, Lee, and Palm Beach Counties as well as Dade, Collier, and Monroe. ISBN 1-56164-262-2 (pb)

Guide to the Lake Okeechobee Area by Bill and Carol Gregware. The first comprehensive guidebook to this area of the state includes a 110-mile hike/bike tour on top of the Herbert Hoover Dike encircling the lake, part of the Florida National Scenic Trail. ISBN 1-56164-129-4 (pb)

Myakka by P.J. Benshoff. What's there to do in Myakka River State Park, the largest state park in Florida? This book takes you on dozens of adventures into this wild area, from shady oak hammocks up into aerial gardens, down the wild and scenic river, and across a variegated canvas of prairies, piney woods, and wetlands. ISBN 1-56164-254-1 (pb)

Sea Kayaking in Florida by David Gluckman. This guide to sea kayaking in Florida for novices and experienced paddlers alike includes information on wildlife, camping, and gear; maps of the Big Bend Sea Grasses Saltwater Paddling Trail; tips on kayaking the Everglades; lists of liveries and outfitters; and more. ISBN 1-56164-071-9 (pb)

Sea Kayaking in the Florida Keys by Bruce Wachob. Florida's lower Keys can be experienced in a kayak as in no other way. Including insider information such as directions to remote launch sites, tips for trip planning, and listings of nearby campsites, dining, and lodging, this guide lists thirteen detailed trip descriptions for kayakers of every skill level. ISBN 1-56164-142-1 (pb)

The Springs of Florida by Doug Stamm. Take a guided tour of Florida's fascinating springs in this beautiful book featuring detailed descriptions, maps, and rare underwater photography. Learn how to enjoy these natural wonders while swimming, diving, canoeing, and tubing. ISBN 1-56164-054-9 (hb); 1-56164-048-4 (pb)

The Surfer's Guide to Florida by Amy Vansant. The first comprehensive guide to the waves of Florida offers locations, swell conditions, and particulars of nearly 200 of Florida's best surfing destinations, including where to park and how to get to the beach, whom you might meet, and inside information on the local scene. ISBN 1-56164-073-5 (pb)